Anglo-Saxon Runes

John M. Kemble

Additional notes and translations
by Bill Griffiths

Anglo-Saxon Books

First Published by Anglo-Saxon Books 1991
Reprinted 1993 1996 2002 2011 2012

Published by
Anglo-Saxon Books
Hereward, Black Bank Road, Little Downham
Ely, Cambridgeshire CB6 2UA, England

Printed by Lightning Source
Australia, England, USA

ISBN 9781898281634

John M. Kemble

John Kemble was born, in 1807, into a famous theatrical family: Fanny Kemble was his sister, Sarah Siddons his aunt. John, however, went to study at Trinity College Cambridge; after attempting to bring about a democratic revolution in Spain, he settled in the 1830s to philological study, associating with Benjamin Thorpe and the brothers Grimm. His work includes the first edition of Beowulf in England, a fine collection of Anglo-Saxon charters in the six-volume *Codex Diplomaticus* set, and an introduction to the history of the period, called *The Saxons in England*. He died in 1857.

His essay 'On Anglo-Saxon Runes' first appeared in the journal *Archaeologia* for 1840; it draws on the work of Wilhelm Grimm, but breaks new ground for Anglo-Saxon studies in his survey of the Ruthwell Cross and the Cynewulf poems. It is an expression both of his own indomitable spirit and of the fascination and mystery of the Runes themselves, making one of the most attractive introductions to the topic.

Illustrations

Publisher's Note

The illustrations are those used in the original work. The arrangement of the rune rows in figures 1-6 and 8-11 have been altered so as to make them larger and easier to read. The rows have been broken into approximately equal length sections.

Notes

Kemble's footnotes are lettered.

Bill Griffiths' footnotes are numbered. Where new material has been inserted into Kemble's text it is marked 'BG', but Kemble's work has not been revised.

The illustrations on pages 68 and 69 (edited versions of figs. 17,18,19) have been added so as to make it easier to compare the different drawings of the Ruthwell Cross.

For further information on Runes and Runic texts, see:

W. C. GRIMM *Ueber Deutsche Runen* (Göttingen, 1821)
R. DEROLEZ *Runica Manuscripta* (Bruges 1953)
R.W.V. ELLIOT *Runes: An Introduction* (Manchester, 1959)
R. I. PAGE *An Introduction to English Runes* (London, 1973)
E. MOLTKE *Runes and their Origin* (Copenhagen, 1985)
S. POLLINGTON *Rudiments of Runelore* (Hockwold, 2002)

There is an interesting article on Kemble by Bruce Dickens in the *Proceedings of the British Academy* vol.25 (1939) pp.51-84

On Anglo-Saxon Runes

The particular object of the following remarks are the Runes of the Anglo-Saxons, whether as to their use in inscriptions, or the manner in which they are introduced into manuscripts. I shall therefore have but little to say of Scandinavian or old Norse characters of the same description, unless by way of illustrating the indigenous alphabet: and indeed these require less attention from us, inasmuch as they have been profoundly and successfully studied by those who had the most right to take an interest in them, the antiquaries of Scandinavia and Iceland.

The characters of the Norwegians, Swedes, Danes and Icelanders are not less distinct from those of the Goths, High and Low Germans, and Anglo-Saxons, than the languages of the several nations which they represented. Unquestionably both the alphabets and the languages are, in the widest philosophical generalization, identical: but exclusive knowledge of the Anglo-Saxon or German Runes would as little enable us to decypher Old Norse inscriptions, as exclusive knowledge of the language of the Edda would enable us to read the Old German Krist, the Old Saxon Hêljand, or the Anglo-Saxon Beôwulf:

Facies non omnibus una,

Nec diversa tamen; qualis decet esse sororum.[1]

These preliminary remarks will not be without service in assisting to explain why my interpretations of certain Anglo-Saxon Runic monuments differ *toto cælo*[2] from those of the learned Danes, who have been so obliging as to attempt to decypher them for us; and to save them this trouble in future, is partly the intention of this paper; especially as there seems to have been a sort of tacit understanding in this country, that the labour and the honour might just as well be left to them; in the propriety of which view it is difficult to concur.

---

[1] "Their external appearance (is) not identical, nor on the other hand (is it) unrelated; (but) such as is fitting of sisters." A quotation from Ovid's *Metamorphoses* 2.14, aptly illustrating the relationship between cognate languages.

[2] Literally, "by the whole sky" i.e. "entirely" (a Latin figure of speech)

Much has been written on the Norse Runes, and of this, very much successfully. The German Runes have been far less fortunate. The only treatises which have fallen under my observation are, -first, a little book published in 1821, under the title Ueber Deutsche Runen, by Wilhelm Carl Grimm, brother and fellow-labourer of James Grimm, the greatest philologist of modern times, and, like James Grimm, now an exile, and martyr to the love of constitutional liberty and respect for the sanctity of an oath.[3] Secondly, an article by the same author in the Wiener-Jahrbücher der Literatur, No.XLIII. containing additions to his former book. As far as these works go, they are no doubt excellent; and were they accessible to all of our countrymen who take an interest in the subject, it would be almost unnecessary to pursue the question further: but as German is as yet by no means so generally understood as it must be by all who pretend to any successful investigation of our national antiquities, I shall take the opportunity at once of stating some of William Grimm's results, and of furnishing him with new matter for a second edition of his book.

When we speak of Runes we intend a certain alphabet or set of alphabets: but in this we attach a very confined and merely conventional signification to the word Rûn, which it did not properly bear among the nations whose letters we denote by it. Its original meaning[4] is strictly that of *mysterium, a secret:* hence the privy counsellor of a prince is called his rûn-wita, *e secretis,* his secretary, the person who knows his secrets (Beôwulf, 1. 2650). And so the verb rŷnan, which is derived directly from it, means, *to whisper, to tell secrets,* a sense which we still retain under the corrupt form to *round* in one's ear. So also Rûna denotes a whisperer; but in its far earlier and truer use, a magician, one who knows or practices secret arts, in which sense it is found in the compound word hel-rûna,

---

[3] The Brothers Grimm associated themselves with the democratic protest against the removal of the constitution of the kingdom of Hanover in 1837. They were deprived of their posts at Göttingen University but found refuge and were able to continue their work first in Cassel then in Berlin.

[4] The word rūn in Old English (and cognate languages) seems to be used in several ways: to mean (a) 'a letter', 'writing', (b) 'a private thought', 'an idea', (c) 'a whisper', 'sound'. Which may be the root meaning, and whether secrecy/mystery are implicit in the word's origin or connotations developed later, cannot easily be determined.

Beôw. 1. 324,[5] (Old Germ. helli-rûno; and similarly Old Germ. helli-rûna, *ars magica*. Docen. 218, b. Glossæ Florentinæ, 982, b.), in the Aliorunæ of Jornanthes, and the Alraun of modern German superstition.

At what period the German tribes first possessed letters of the alphabet, whether invented by themselves or derived from some other race, in times of which history is silent, it would perhaps be hopeless, and now would certainly be useless to inquire. It is enough for my purpose that they had them, when those tribes first came under the notice of the Romans. Some evidence of this will be adduced below: for the present it will be enough to call attention to a passage of Tacitus, principally for the purpose of explaining it. Speaking of the priestesses or prophetesses of the Germans, he says; "Sed et olim *Auriniam* et complures alias venerati sunt, non adulatione, nec tanquam facerent deas." (Germ. III.)[6] Now this word *Aurinia,*which Tacitus naturally took to be the proper name of a woman, and which has always been so construed, is in fact no more than the general appellative of a prophetess or sorceress, in short *Alrynia*; according to the passage already alluded to in Jornanthes, who relates that Filimer expelled from his kingdom, "quasdam magas mulieres, quas patrio sermone Aliorunnas cognominant."[7] (Vide J. Grimm, Deut. Myth. p. 227.) In confirmation of which it may be added, that Veleda, the name of Civilis's high-hearted associate, may also be only a general appellative, closely connected etymologically with the old Norse Vavlu (Völu), a prophetess. But if in the time of Tacitus,[8] the general or even the particular name Alrynia was found, it is sufficient evidence of the existence of that from which the word was derived, namely, Rûn, both the thing itself and its especial use for magical purposes.

<hr>

[5] Kemble throughout numbers verse lines by counting half-lines. To correlate with a modern edition, divide Kemble's number by two. Also, throughout, he uses the circumflex accent to denote a long vowel in Old English.

[6] "But once also they venerated Aurinia and several other female beings, (but) not with servile adulation, nor so as to make of them goddesses."

[7] "certain female enchantresses, who in the native tongue they call Aliorunnae."

[8] Whether examples of this sort from the 1st century AD relate to runes remains an open question.

But still, at this period, and till far later times, the knowledge of the letters and their powers was confined to certain classes only of the people. History and tradition assure us that they were known to that family which furnished the Teutonic tribes with priests and kings, and to both old and young among the women - the sacred sex. Yet to many even of these, and to all but these, they were in themselves mysterious and awful symbols: and hence the name given to them, viz. Rûn-stafas, *mysterious staves,* (Beôw. 1. 3388) answering to the later Bôcstafas, or Latin characters, the modern German Buchstaben.

In the times when there was neither pen, ink nor parchment, the bark of trees and smooth surfaces of wood or soft stone were the usual depositories of these symbols: hence the word Wrîtan, now *to write,* but whose primary signification was to *cut* or *carve* (Beôw. 1. 5406). As Brynolf Svenonius remarks, "Runas incidere lignis, pro effectus varietate, variis et aliis generibus rerum, solens erat. Lignum porro hoc κεχαραγμενον, breviculum exiguum ferè, *Runakeffle* dicunt, quasi Claviculum Runicum dicas, et *Rista Runer,* incidere Runas, propriè, vel ut Saxo, insculpere; non scribere, aut pingere, dixeris."[9] (in Stephanius, Notæ Uberior. in Saxon. Grammatic. p. 46.) Hence also Stafas, the smooth sticks on which they were cut; and hence even the word Bôc, *book,* which recalls the beechen tablets in which they were inscribed.

The earliest runes, then, were cut in surfaces of stone and wood.[10] The former case would comprise inscriptions on rocks, gravestones and weapons: the latter would be confined to the wooden tablets or sticks used in casting lots and divination.

The concurrent testimony of tradition and the evidence of actual fact, assure us that throughout Europe short inscriptions were in use commemorative of great public events, or of distinguished individuals.

---

[9] "It was customary to engrave runes on pieces of wood, with different effects in different cases. Indeed, such wood, (in Greek) 'kecharagmenon', i.e. 'short' or 'scanty', they call Runakeffle, 'a small runic key', and (they say) Rista Runer, 'to inscribe runes' literally, or as in Saxo 'to engrave'; you do not talk of 'writing' or 'painting' (them)."

[10] The straight and angular shapes of runes, with vertical and diagonal but not horizontal strokes, suggests the grained face of wood to be the original material involved; that the material written on defined the subject matter must be uncertain though.

One or two of these will occupy our attention presently, being yet extant in Anglo-Saxon Runes: while the immense number of *Bautasteinar* and other sculptured monuments in Scandinavia renders any further notice of them unnecessary. That weapons of stone and even of metal were marked with Runes in Scandinavia, is also certain: and the sword of stone with which Beôwulf slew the Grendel's mother, is described to have been furnished with them (l. 3388). Its hilt was marked with Runestaves, declaring "by whom it had first been fashioned in the olden time, when the proud giants perished." Brynhildr teaches Sigurdr to cut the Sigrunar on the hilt of his sword.

> Sigrúnar þu skalt kunna
> ef þú vilt sigr hafa
> ok rista á hialti hiörs.
> Sumar á vetrimom
> sumar á valbavstom
> ok nefna tvistvar Týr.11

(Brynhild, Quid. 1. 6.) Vide also, Fôr Skyrnis, 32 and 36.

The use of lots in divination, by the Germans, is known to us from several passages, forming a chain of evidence from the earliest down to the latest periods. Some of these may be cursorily mentioned here.

> Quum ex captivis quæreret Cæsar, quamobrem Ariovistus prælio non decertaret, hanc reperiebat causam; quod apud Germanos ea consuetudo esset, ut matres familiæ eorum sortibus et divinationibus declararent, utrum prælium committi ex usu esset, nec ne.12

(De Bello Gallico, 1. 50.)

---

11 "Victory-runes you must learn if you wish to obtain victory, and cut (them) on the hilt of (your) sword; some on the ?blade-channel, some on the ?blade-ridge; and name, twice, Týr." From the *Sigrdrifu-mál.*

12 "When Caesar enquired of the captives why Ariovistus had not decided on battle, he obtained this explanation: that among the Germans it was the custom that the matrons of the tribe would, by means of (casting) lots and of divinations, discover whether it would be advantageous to go to battle or not."

Again,

> Is se præsente, de se ter sortibus consultum dicebat, utrum igni statim necaretur, an in aliud tempus reservaretur: sortium benefico se esse incolumem.[13]   *(De Bell. Gall. 1. 53.)*

So much for the Germans when they first burst upon the Roman empire. In the eighth century we find the same custom prevailing upon the remote shores of Friesland. Alcuin, in his Life of Willibrord, who died in 739, after relating how the saint and his companions defiled the sacred wells, and slew the sacred cattle of the god Fosite, continues:

> Quod pagani intuentes arbitrabantur, eos vel in furorem verti, vel etiam veloci morte perire; quos cum nil mali cernebant pati, stupore perterriti regi tamen Râdbodo quod viderant factum retulerunt. Qui nimio furore succensus, in sacerdotem dei vivi suorum injurias deorum ulcisci cogitabat, et per tres dies semper tribus vicibus sortes suo more mittebat, et numquam damnatorum sors, deo vero defendente suos, super servum dei aut aliquem ex suis cadere potuit; nec nisi unus tantum ex sociis, sorte monstratus, martyrio coronatus est.[14]

It is very clear from the circumstances that, in no one of these cases, a mere casting of lots is intended: they were obviously auguries or divinations.[15] And such unquestionably were the following, although Beda does not expressly say so: speaking of the old Saxons, or Saxons of the Continent, he observes -

---

[13] "He said that in his own presence (an answer) was sought three times concerning him by (the casting of) lots, whether he should be immediately killed by fire or held over until another time: by the lucky chance of the lots he survived."

[14] "Seeing that, the pagans believed they (i.e. the Christians) had been turned mad and were likely to perish a swift death (by the vengence of the gods); when they perceived no harm to have come to them, themselves shocked by the wonder (of it), they reported what they had seen happen to their king, Radbodus. He, roused to a pitch of fury, intended to avenge the insults to his gods on the priest of the living God, and thrice on each of the three days he cast lots, according to their custom, yet never could he make fall the lot of condemnation against the servant of God or any of his (friends), (for) the true God defended his own; nor indeed did any of his companions ever after that receive the crown of martyrdom, (thus bearing out what) the lot had shown."

[15] As stated here, the relationship between the casting of lots and runes as such remains unclear. Examples of the linkage between runes and magic (on page 16 etc, below) come from a rather later period.

Non enim habent regem iidem antiqui Saxones, sed satrapas plurimos suæ genti præpositos; qui, ingruente belli articulo, mittunt æqualiter sortes, et quemcumque sors ostenderit, hunc tempore belli ducem omnes sequuntur, huic obtemperant: peracto autem bello, rursum æqualis potentiæ omnes fiunt satrapæ.[16] (Hist. Eccl. v. ch. 10.)

The legend of Saint Andrew, in the Vercelli Codex, describes a similar casting of lots, with the very important notice that it was done in the presence of heathen gods:

Þâ wæs eallgeador	Then was altogether
tô þâm þingstede	in the public place
þeôd gesamnod.	the people collected.
Leton him þâ betweonum	They let among them
tân[a] wîsian,	the twig decide,
hwylcne hyra ǽrest	which of them first
ôðrum sceôlde,	unto the others should,
tô fôddurþege,	for a supply of food,
feores ongyldan.	his life give up.
Hluton hellcræftum	They cast lots with hellish craft
hǽðen-gyldum,	before the heathen gods,
teledon betwinum.	they reckoned among themselves.
Ðâ se tân gehwearp	Then went the twig[17]
efne ofer ǽnne	even over one
ealdgesîða,	of the old comrades,
se wæs uðweota	who was a councillor
eorla dûguðe,	to the power of the warriors,
heriges on ore.	a leader in the host.
Hraðe syððan wearð	Quickly was he then
fetorwræsnum fæst	fast in fetters
feores orwêna."	despairing of life.

16 "For they still have no king, just as the old Saxons (did not), but several governors put in power over their tribe; these, when a time of war occurs, all cast lots, and whoever the lot picks out, him they all follow as leader for the duration of the warfare (and) him they obey: but when the war is finished, they are each governers again of equal rank."

a So, Old Norse Tein.

17 The turning (dipping?) of the twig suggests a process like water-divining. The passage quoted is lines 1097-1107 in modern editions; there are minor inaccuries in the text Kemble quotes, as with others in this booklet; but satisfactory editions of Old English texts were seldom produced in his day.

A still later authority gives us additional information. La3amon tells us, that, when Brutus's mother was found to be with child, lots were cast to discover what fortune was reserved for him:

Vnder3etene weren þe þinges
þat þeo wimon was mid childe.
þa sende Ascanius,
þe was lauerd and dux,
after heom 3end þat lond
þe cuþen dweomerlakes song.
Witen he wolde
þurh þa wiþercraftes
wat þing hit were
þat þeo wimon hefde on wombe.
Heo wrpen heore leoten,
þe scucke wes bitweonan;
heo funden on þen crefte
carefule leoðes,
þet þeo wimon was mid ane sune,
þat wes a selcuð bearn.
. . . .
þo leoten weren iworpen,
and swa hit al iwearð.[18]

That spells and magical chants, (*carmina diabolica,* þe scucke wes bitweonan) accompanied the ceremony of casting lots, whether in the time of Ariovistus or of Râdbod, there can be no question. In short, so undoubtedly magical is the whole process, that the Old German dialect has the one word *hliozzari,* a caster of lots, only in the sense of a magician. As an illustration of the "dweomerlakes song" in the last cited passage, and as a proper introduction to the next part of my argument, I must call attention to a passage in Saxo Grammaticus.

[18] "Perceived were the facts that the woman was with child. Then sent Ascanius, who was lord and duke, for them throughout that land who knew the chant of sorcery. He wanted to know through the black arts what sort of being it was that the woman had in her womb. They cast their lots - the devil was in it all; they found by that skill doleful news, that the woman was carrying a son, who was (to be) a prodigy...... The lots were cast, and so it all turned out." The passage is from Layamon's *Brut,* verses 266-280 in Madden's edition; the text dates from the early C13th.

Speaking of Hardgrepa, he says, - "Quo comite susceptum iter ingressa, penatibus forte pernoctatura succedit, quorum defuncti hospitis funus mæstis ducebatur exequiis. Ubi magicæ speculationis officio superum mentem rimari cupiens, diris admodum carminibus ligno insculptis, iisdemque lingua defuncti per Haddingum suppositis, hac voce eum horrendum auribus carmen edere coegit."[19] (P. 11, Ed. Stephanii.)

On this the excellent Bishop Brynolf Svenonius whom I have already cited, observes, "Nullus dubito quin Runas Saxo intellectas velit."[20] In this I agree entirely, for unquestionably, in this case, as in that of the casting of lots, the tablets were invariably inscribed with Runes, from whose power the result of the ceremony depended. This is not denied, as far as the Scandinavians are concerned; it is therefore now only necessary to show that it is true of the German tribes also. Hrabanus Maurus, writing at the beginning of the ninth century, says (Ed. Colon. 1626, ii. 334):-

> Litteras quippe quas utuntur Marcomanni, quos nos Nordmannos vocamus, infra scriptas habemus; a quibus originem qui Theodiscam loquuntur linguam trahunt: cum quibus carmina sua, incantationesque ac divinationes significare procurant, qui adhuc paganis ritibus involvuntur.[21]

He then gives his Marcomannic or Norman Runic Alphabet. The Cotton MS. Tib. D. xviii. furnishes another copy of them, with slight variations in the forms and names of the Runes; and with the following observation:-

---

[19] "When she (Hardgrepa) had begun the accepted journey, in the company of that noble (Hadding), she came by chance, (needing) night-shelter, upon some dwellings whose dead owner's funeral was being conducted with mournful obsequies. There, wishing to question the intention of the gods by means of magical interrogation, she carved some very dreadful incantations on wood, and got Hadding to place these under the tongue of the corpse, and so forced him with this (alien?) voice to issue speech, (in tones) terrible to hear." From Book 1, chapter 22 of Saxo Grammaticus' *History of the Danes*

[20] "I do not doubt but that Saxo intended Runes to be meant."

[21] "Indeed the letters the Marcomanni use, who we call Northmen, we have written out below; to these they that speak the German tongue attribute the origin (of their writing?); with these, those who are still involved in pagan practice make the effort to transcribe their songs, incantations and spells."

Hæc etenim literarum figuræ in gente Nortmannorum feruntur primitus inventæ, quibus ob carminum eorum memoriam et incantationum uti adhuc dicuntur: quibus et Rûnstafas nomen imposuerunt; ob id, ut reor, quod hiis res absconditas vicissim scriptitando aperiebant.[b] [22]

Who then are these Marcomanni or Nordmanni? The inhabitants of Holstein, Stormaria and Ditmarsh, the Nordalbingii or Saxons north of the Elbe, and the progenitors of our own Anglo-Saxon population. This will appear from a few passages taken at random, from ancient German chronicles:-

"Nortliudi trans Albim sedentes."[23] - (Ann. Laurish. A.D. 796.) where the Annales Einhardi call them Saxones Transalbiani." - (Pertz. i. 184-5-6.)

"Inde iter agens partibus Albiæ, in ipso itinere omnes Bargengauenses et multi de Nordliudis baptizati sunt."[24] (Ann. Tiliens. A.D. 780. Pertz. i. 221.)

"Ad recipiendos qui de Nortliudis venerant Saxones." (Ann. Tiliens. A.D. 799. Pertz. i. 221.) "Quosdam Saxones de Nordliudis recipiendos."[25] (Ann. Einhard. A.D. 799. Pertz. i. 186)

"Gens quædam Aquilonaris, quam plerique Nordalbincos, alii usitatius Normannos vocant."[26] - (Fulcuin. De Gest. Abbat. Lobiens. cap. xvi. in Achery Spicileg. 735)

---

[b] It is an interesting coincidence that in Welsh the Alphabet was called "The lot of the Bards," Coelbren y Beirdd.

[22] "For these forms of letters are said first to have been devised among the race of Northmen, (and) they are said to use them still for the purpose of recording their songs and incantations; and to them they have given the name of Runes; for this reason, as I think, that through them they make clear secret things by repeated writing." This last assertion might be a sort of mild sarcasm, or imply an authentic activation through ritual repetition.

[23] "North-nation living beyond the Elbe."

[24] "Journeying from there to the regions of the Elbe, on the same journey all the Thuringians and many of the Northmen were baptized." - reading Bardengauenses.

[25] "For bringing in Saxons who came from the Northmen." and "Certain Saxons brought in from the Northmen."

[26] "A certain northern people, who many call Nordalbinci, or more usually, Normanni."

16

"Fuerunt parentes mandato ejus plebes Holzatorum, Sturmariorum, et Marcomannorum. Vocantur autem usitato more Marcomanni gentes undecumque collectæ quæ Marcam incolunt."[27]
(Helmold. Chron. Slav. in Leibnitz. Script. Rer. Brunsw. ii. 593.)

"Saxonum populus quidam quos claudit ab Austro Albia seiunctim positos aquilonis ad axem: Hos Northalbingos patrio sermone vocamus."[28]
(Poema de Gest. Caroli Magni, A.D. 798. Hist. Franc. Script. ii.160. Ed. Paris, 1636.)

These Marcomannic Runes I shall hereafter show do resemble the Anglo-Saxon, and do not resemble the Norse Runes, very closely. We have, therefore, evidence not only that the Germans attributed to these letters the powers which the Scandinavians believed them to possess, but that, of the Germans, the immediate progenitors of the Anglo-Saxons did so. A further point of coincidence in the belief of the two races lies in this; that both attributed the invention of the Runes to Odinn or Wôden. In the Icelandic Runa Capitul, Odinn says, "Nam ek up Runar" (I invented Runes).[c] In the prose Anglo-Saxon dialogue of Salomon and Saturn, and also in that of Adrian and Ritheus, the question is asked, "Saga me, hwâ wrât bôcstafas ǣrest?" (Tell me, who first wrote letters?) To which the answer is, "Ic ðe secge, Mercurius se gigant," (I tell thee, Mercurius the giant:) in other words, and according to the *interpretatio Romana*[29] , Wôden the God: for Wôden is Mercurius, as it is plainly stated by Paulus Diaconus (i. 9.) "Wodan sanè, quem adjecta litera Gwodan dixerunt, ipse est qui apud Romanos Mercurius dicitur, et ab universis Germaniæ gentibus ut deus adoratur."[30] And again by the still earlier

[27] "Their parents were, by their own account, people of the Holzati [in Holstein], Sturmarii [in Stormaria] and Marcomanni. But by common usage they are all called the Marcomanni, a people brought together from many places and who worship Marca."
[28] "That race of Saxons whom the Elbe bounds on the south, (and who are) placed apart in the region of the north: these we call the Northalbingi in the native tongue."
[c] See also the following stanzas of the Runa Capitul, particularly the Brynhild. Quid. I. 13.
[29] "the Roman version".
[30] "Indeed Woden, whom with a prefixed letter they call Gwoden, is the one who is called Mercury among the Romans, and he is worshipped as a god by all the German peoples."

Jonas of Bobbio, who writes: "Illi aiunt, deo suo Wodano, quem Mercurium vocant alii, se velle litare."[31] Hence also it is that "dies Mercurii" is Wôdnesdæg, and that Cæsar could say, Mercury was the principal God of the Teutons.

I have shown that the German Saxons shared with the Northmen, or Scandinavians, the belief in the magical properties of Runes. But even till a late period the same thing may be said of the Anglo-Saxons: Christianity, though it laboured successfully to destroy these superstitions, and so successfully as to make it difficult for us to say to what extent they had prevailed, has yet not been able to eradicate all traces of their former existence. Beda, relating the adventures of a Saxon nobleman, made prisoner in the battle between Ecgfrith of Northumberland and Aethilred of Mercia, A.D. 679, and whose bonds fell off whenever his brother, who supposed him dead, celebrated mass for his soul, - adds that his captor believed the miracle to be caused by his having magical Runes: "Interea comes qui eum tenebat, mirari et interrogare cœpit quare ligari non posset; an forte *literas solutorias,* de qualibus fabulæ ferunt, apud se haberet, propter quas ligari non posset."[32] (Hist. Eccl. iv. 22.) The Saxon translation renders Literas solutorias, by âlŷsendlîce Rûne.[d]   Again, in Beôwulf, a person commencing a flyting, which was likely to produce a quarrel, is said to "unbind the Rune of war," onband beadurûne, (l. 996.) In the poetical dialogue of Salomon and Saturn, a very interesting passage occurs, which retains the feeling of the old superstition, although the word rûn is not found in it. According to the habitual practice of Christian times, the old heathen beliefs and usages have sunk down into diabolical illusions - mere results of the agency of the devil: among other things it is said of the fiends,-

Hwîlum hîe gefeteraÞ	By whiles they fetter
fǣges monnes honda,	the hands of the doomed, (fey)
gehefegaÞ Þonne he	they make them heavy when he

[31] "They say they wish to sacrifice to their god Woden, whom others call Mercury."

[32] "Meanwhile the officer who held him began to marvel and inquire why he could not be bound; did he perhaps have about him the letters of unbinding, of which sort of thing stories are told, and on account of which he could not be tied up."

[d] So Odinn says in the Runna Capitul, - "That kann ek fiorda, ef mer fyrdar bera bavnd at boglimom. sva ek gel at ek ganga ma, sprettr mer af fotumm fiöturr, en af havndum hapt." ("This I can do fourthly: if my foemen lay bonds on my limbs, I can so chant that I go free: spring off my feet the fetters and off my hands the shackles." From the *Háva-mál* or *Words of the High One* BG.)

æt hilde sceall	ought in war
wið lâðwerud	against the hostile troop
lifes tiligan:	to provide for his life:
awrîtað hîe on his wæpne	they write upon his weapon
wælnota heâp,	a crowd of fatal notes,
bealwe bôcstafas:	deadly letters:
bill forscrîfað,	they wear out the bill,
meces mærðo."	the glory of the sword.e [33]

We can now understand why the Runes, which were the invention of Wôden, the secret character of the priests and prophetesses, the means of pagan augury, and the necessary adjuncts to the *Carmina diabolica* of the heathen, were proscribed by the Christian priesthood in every part of Europe; and why these laboured with an energy apparently disproportioned to the necessity of the case, to introduce the Greek or Latin characters, together with, and almost as a part of, Christianity. The Runes, in this view, are the indigenous Pagan alphabet, as contrasted with the Greek characters introduced by Ulfilas among the Goths, and called Mæsogothic; the Latin characters introduced, probably by Augustine, into England, and called Anglo-Saxon; misnomers which, in spite of the doctrine and practice of the best scholars at home and abroad, still throw difficulties in the way of publishing our ancient monuments, by keeping up a respect for the barbarous mediæval forms[34] of Greek and Roman letters, and saddling both editors and readers with a trouble and an expense not compensated for by any corresponding advantage.

The hostility of the Christian Missionaries to the Runes, if it requires any corroboration, may be proved by the assertion of the learned Bishop, before cited; Svenonius says,-

---

[e] So Odinn says in the Runa Capitul, - "Eggiar ek deyfi minna Andskota bitaþ þeim vapn ne velir." ("I can blunt my enemies' swords: their weapons will bite (no more) than [reading an for ne] sticks." From the *Háva-mál* or *Words of the High One.* BG.)

[33] The lines of Old English poetry quoted are *Solomon and Saturn* 158-163

[34] Kemble seems to be attacking the use of insular minuscule letter forms in the printing of Old English, which was standard into the middle of the 19th century. As such manuscript letter-forms are not truly "insular" but Roman in origin, one might just as well (he seems to say) use normal modern lettering - as he does for all quotations in this work.

19

Videlicet maximè a Christianis est laboratum, ut scripta et monumenta vetustatis gentilis penitus obruerentur, æterna oblivionis humo sepulta. Quia videlicet persuasum erat, quamdiu vestigium cultus et characterum antiquiorum, hominum animis obversaret, negotium conversionis non satis procedere, hominibus ad pristinas præstigias pronis et facilibus. Ideoque, ne obstrueret veritatis luminibus potestas tenebrarum, nec tamen ferret rude vulgus subtiliorem, quàm pro suo captu, usus ab abusu distinctionem, et accederet zelus verbi ministrorum pontificiis consuetus, et cupido Romanam ecclesiam omnibus modis propagandi, literas Romanas, ut sanctiores, Normannicis, tanquam gentili superstitione pollutis, commutare consultum visum est. De quo facto meum judicium non requiri ut certò scio, ita libenter contineo.[35] (Stephanius, Not. Uber. p. 46.)

The authority of two such estimable prelates as our author and Esaias Tegner will excuse a layman for lamenting that the ancient faith of our forefathers had not fairer play. But this hostility being once admitted, how are we to account for the undeniable fact, that at the very earliest period these characters were used in England for Christian inscriptions? It seems to me that the only way of solving this intricate problem, is to assume, that the earliest converts were the priests themselves; which fact, astounding as it is, is rendered probable by positive evidence. If this were

---

[35] "Clearly there was considerable effort (expended) by the Christians to obliterate entirely writings and monuments of the native past, (and) bury them in the everlasting grave of oblivion. For clearly they were convinced that as long as any trace of the culture and ancient signs obtruded on the minds of men, the business of conversion could not properly proceed, with men inclined and liable (to return) to their former errors. At the same time, so that the power of the darkness should not obstruct the rays of truth, nor on the other hand to make the common people too clever, above their capacity, a distinction of 'use' from 'abuse', and (so that) zeal for the word of the ministers, customary among the priests, should grow, and that enthusiasm for bringing the Roman Church to all minds grow too, it seemed wise to substitute Roman letters, as holier, for the (letters of the) Northmen, polluted as it were, by native superstition. On which point, my pronouncement is hardly required that I know it for certain (but) I freely maintain it." In justice, we should note that Christian scribes adopted two runic characters ('thorn' for 'th' and 'wyn' for 'w') into their Roman script; that runes were freely used on Christian monuments; and that indeed such fragments as we do have of pagan literature owe their preservation to being written down in the monastic scriptoria. The Church doubtless suppressed, but like any institution, also instincively preserved.

the case, they who knew what the Runes really were, might have the less scruple in using them, with or without the Roman characters. And, as nearly every inscription we have must be referred to Northumberland, we find this the more intelligible, when we bear in mind, that before the close of the eighth century Northumberland was more advanced in civilization than any other portion of Teutonic Europe.

With these general and very cursory remarks upon Runes in general, I proceed to the immediate business of this paper, viz. the Anglo-Saxon Runic alphabets and inscriptions. I have said that the Marcomannic Runes mentioned by Hrabanus Maurus were in fact identical with those of the Anglo-Saxons. This will readily appear from a comparison of the characters themselves; for which purpose I have given the alphabets from Hrabanus, and the Cotton MS. Tib. D. xviii. (Figs. 1 & 2) Other copies of this alphabet, some distinguished by important variations, may be seen in Hickes.Thes. Gram. Isl. Tab. I. et II. 5. 12. Wormius de Lit. Runic. p. 46. 49. Goldast. Antiq. Aleman. Tom. II. pt. i. Lazius de Migrat. Gent. p. 645. Trithemius Polygraph. Lib VI. p. 594. Purchas, Perigrin. I. cap. xvii. p. 183: and lastly, in Wilhelm Grimm's Book on German Runes.

In order to point out clearly the relation which the Marcomannic Runes bear to our own, I proceed to give copies of two or three alphabets, which, to the best of my knowledge, have never been published in this country; and some of which I have copied myself from the MSS. on the Continent; premising that Anglo-Saxon alphabets, of very different degrees of accuracy, are to be found in Hickes, Thes. Gram. Island. Tab. II. 2,3,6,8,9,10. Gram. Anglo-Sax. Thes. p. 136.

No. 1. (Fig. 3.) is from a MS. of Isidor, at Brussels, No. 155: it is printed for the first time in Archivarius Mone's Quellen und Forschungen.

No. 2. (Fig. 4.) from a MS. in the Conventual Library of St. Gallen. No. 270. fol. 52.

No. 3. (Fig. 5.) from the same MS and page.

No. 4. (Fig. 6.) from a MS. at Munich; printed by W. C. Grimm, in the Wiener Jahrbücher, &c. XLIII.

No. 5. (Fig 7.) from a MS. at Vienna. Salisb. No. 140, (formerly No. 71,) printed in the same periodical.

No. 6. (Fig. 8.) from a MS. at St. Gallen, No. 878,   f. 321; printed in W. C. Grimm, Ueber Deutsche Runen. Tab. II.

No. 7. (Fig. 9.) from a MS. of Isidor at Paris; from the same work.

No. 8. (Fig. 10.) from a MS. in the Harl. Collect. No. 3017.

Fig. 1

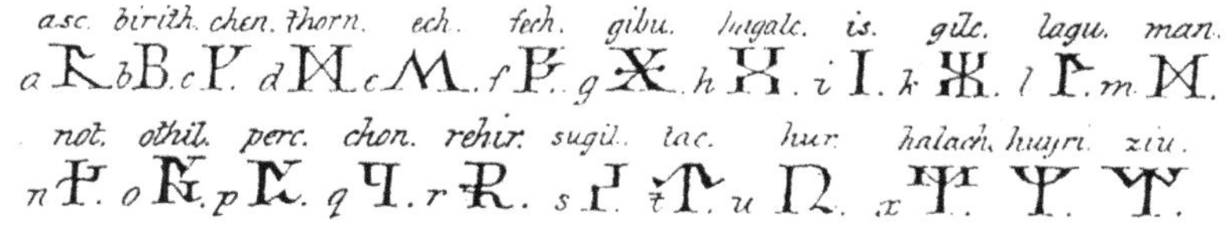

asc. birith. chen. thorn. ech. fech. gibu. hagale. is. gile. lagu. man.

not. othil. perc. chon. rehir. sugil. tac. hur. halach. huyri. ziu.

Fig. 2

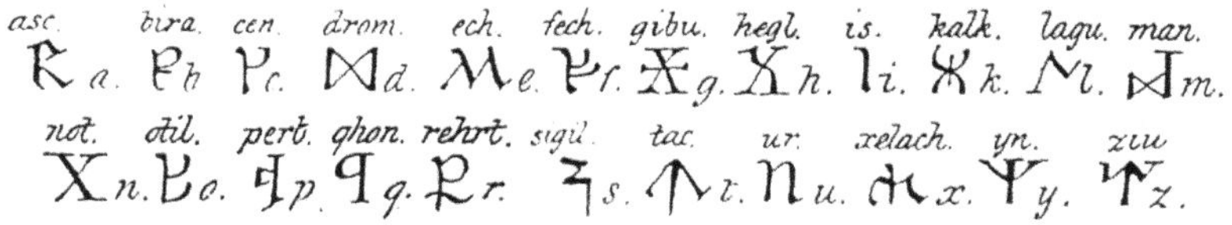

asc. bira. cen. drom. ech. fech. gibu. hegl. is. kalk. lagu. man.

not. otil. perb. qhon. rehrt. sigil. tac. ur. xelach. yn. ziu.

Fig. 3

fech. ur. thorn. os. rad. ken. geuo. uung. hagal. not. is. iar. hio. per. ilix. sigil.
f. u. th. o. r. c. g. uu. h. n. i. ger. ih. p. il. s.

ti. berc. hec. man. lag. hinc. dag. othil. as. e.
t. b. e. m. l. in. d. oe. a. eo. k. g.

Fig.4

feh. uur. dorn. oos. rot. cen. gebc. huun. hagal. nod. iis. ger. ih. perd.
f. u. th. oo. r. c. g. uu. h. n. i. j. k. p.

elix. sigi. ti. berg. eh. man. lago. inc. dag. odil. ac. osc. yur. der.
x. s. t. b. e. m. m. i. n. i. o. a. aa. y. z.

23

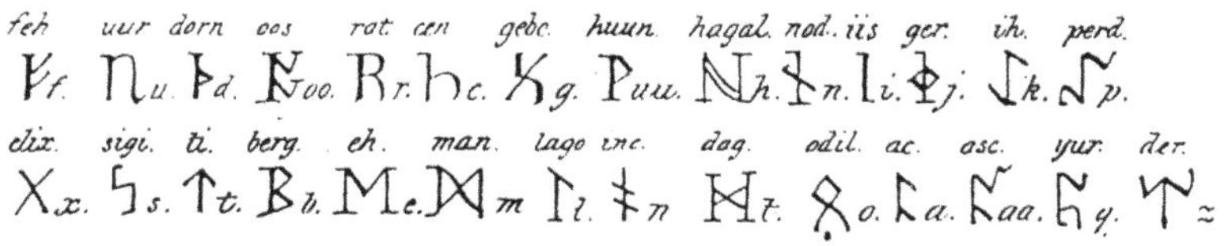

Fig. 5

a a b c d d e f g g g h i k l

m n o o p p q r s t t u x z

Fig. 6

ng.cür. beric. cen. dai. eh. feh. geuo. heih. is. ker. lago.

man. pat. os. perd. cen. rat. sil. tir. ur. elcd. uyr.

Fig. 7

ffe.   u.   d.   o.   r.   c.   j.   uu.   h.   n.   i.   ij.   ieth.
p.   lel.z   s.   t.   b.   e.   m.   l.   net.g   d.   oc.   a.
ae.   ea.   y.   a · e : i ? o :: u ::

Fig. 8

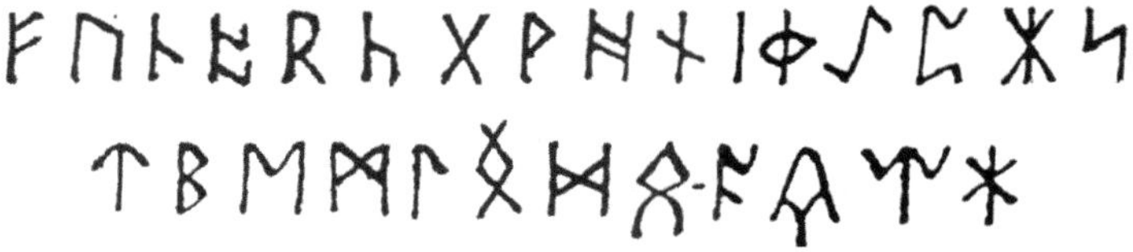

Fig. 9

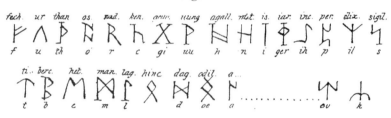

fech. ur than os. rad. ken. gini. uung agall. niit. is. iar. inc. per. elix. sigil.

f u th o r c gi uu h n i ger th p il s

ti.. berc. het. man. lag. hinc. dag. odil. a...

t b e m l d oe a .... ov k

Fig. 10

Fig. 11

feoh ur dorn os. rad. cen: gyfu uen.p. hægl. nyd. is. ger.

f u d o r c g uu h n i g

eoh peord edhx. sigel tir beorc. eh. deg lagu ing. ebel.

eo p x s t b e m l ing oe

man aug ac. asc. yr. tar. tir. ear. eweort. stan. gar.

m a ac y io ear q h st. g

These will supply us with sufficient materials for any investigation in which Anglo-Saxon Runes only can possibly be concerned. The most instructive, however, of all the documents we possess on the subject, is the poem printed by Hickes, Thes. Gram. Anglo-Sax.[36] p. 135, from a MS. now unhappily lost. As I know of no English translation of this, and William Grimm's version is inaccurate in one or two points, I shall give one of my own. It is to be observed, that the first word of every stanza[37] is represented by the Rune of which the word itself was the name. These, for convenience sake, I have omitted in the text, where they stand one under another; and have had them lithographed. one after another, in No. 9. (Fig. 11.) The only changes I have made in the text, are one or two grammatical corrections, as *um* for *un*, &c.-

"FEOH byð frôfur fira gehwylcum; sceal ðeâh manna gehwylc miclum hit dǽlan, gif he wile for Drihtne dômes hleôtan.	Money is a consolation to every man; yet shall every man liberally distribute it, if he will that, before God, honour shall fall to his lot.
"UR byð ânmod and oferhyrned, felafrecne deôr feohteð mid hornum, mǽre môrstapa: ðæt môdig wuht.	Bull[38] is fierce and horned above, the very bold beast fighteth with horns, a mighty stepper over the moors: that is a courageous creature.

[36] Hickes' *Thesaurus* was published in two volumes, 1703-5; he printed and thus preserved several Old English texts the manuscripts of which were subsequently lost when the Cottonian library was damaged by fire in 1731.

[37] In fact the manuscript probably contained a space for the rune at the start of each stanza: the runes in the *Thesaurus* printing were likely supplied by Hickes from elsewhere. See Hempl's article in *Modern Philology* 1 (1903-4).

[38] To be exact, the aurochs, or Bos primigenius.

"ÐORN byð þearle scearp
þegna gehwylcum,
anfengys yfel,
ungemetum rêðe
manna gehwylcum
ðe mid him resteð.

Thorn is very sharp
to every man,
bad to take hold of,
immeasurably severe
to every man
that resteth with him.

"Os byð odfruma
ǽlcere sprǽce,
wîsdômes wraðu,
und witena frôfur,
and eorla gehwâm
eâdnys and tôhẙht.

Mouth[39] is the origin
of every speech,
the support of wisdom,
and comfort of councillors,
and to every man
blessing and confidence.

"RAD byð on recyde
rinca gehwylcum
sêfte and swîðhwæt,
ðâm ðe sitteð on ûfan
meare mægenheardum
ofer milpaðas.

Saddle is in the house
to every man
soft and very bold,
for him that sitteth upon
the very strong horse,
over the mile paths.

"CEN byð cwicera gehwâm
cûð on fŷre,
blâc and beorhtlîc
byrneð oftust,
ðær hî æðelingas
inne restað

Torch is to all living
well known on fire,
pale and bright
it oftenest burneth,
where the nobles
rest them within.

[39] Though Os could refer to the Æsir or northern gods, the Old English poem
interprets the word by its Latin meaning, 'mouth'.

27

"GIFU gumena byð
gleng and herenys,
wraðu and weorðscype,
and wræcna gehwâm
âr and ætwist
ðe byð ôðra leâs.

Gift is of men
glory and exaltation,
support and honour,
and to every one
honour and sustenance,
that hath no other.

WEN ne brûceð
ðe can weana lyt,
sâres and sorge
and him sylfa hæfð
blæd and blýsse
and eâc byrga geniht.

Hope he needeth not
that hath but little want,
soreness and sorrow,
and hath himself
increase and bliss
and also the enjoyment of borrows.

"HÆGL byð hwîtust corna
hwyrft hit of heofones lyfte,
wealcað hit windes scuras,
worðeð hit tô wætere syððan.

Hail is whitest of grains,
it sweepeth from the lift of heaven.
the showers of the wind whirl it about,
after it turneth to water.

"NYD byð nearu on breôste
niða bearnum,
weorðeð heô ðeâh
oft tô helpe
and tô hæ̂le gehwæðre
gif hî his hlystað æ̂ror.

Need[40] is narrow in the breast
for the sons of men,
yet doth it become
often a help
and safety for any one
if they sooner attend to it.

"IS byð oferceald,
ungemetum slidor;
glisnað glæshluttur
gimmum gelîcust
flôr forste geworuht,
fæger ansŷne.

Ice is over-cold,
immeasurably slippery;
glittereth bright as glass
likest unto gems,
the plain wrought with frost
fair to behold.

---

[40] i.e. 'neediness', 'lack', 'hardship'.

"GER byð gumena hiht,
ðonne God læteð,
hâlig heofones cyning,
hrûsan syllan
beorhte blæda
beornum and þearfum.

Year is the hope of men,
when God letteth,
the holy king of heaven,
the earth give
her bright increase
to rich and poor.

"EOH bið ûtan
unsmeðe treôw,
heard, hrusan fæst,
hyrde fŷres,
wyrtrumum underwreðŷd,
wyn on êðle.

Yew is outwardly
an unsmooth tree,
hard, fast in the earth,
the shepherd of fire,
twisted beneath with roots,
a pleasure on the land.

"PEORÐ byð symble
plega and hlehter
wlancum, ðær
wîgan sittað
on beôrsele
bliðe æt somne.

Chessman[41] is ever
play and laughter
to the proud, where
warriors sit
in the beer-hall
blithe together.

"EOLHX secg eardað
oftust on fenne,
weaxeð on wætere,
wundað grimme,
blôde breneð
beorna gehwylcne
ðe him æ̂nigne
onfeng gedêð.

Sedge[42] hath dwelling
oftest in the fen,
waxeth in water,
grimly woundeth,
burneth in the blood,
every man
that any way
toucheth it.

---

[41] Though 'chessman' fits the sense of the verse well, it cannot be proved to be the meaning of 'peorð' - conjecture as to what this rune means (if anything) still continues.
[42] Eolh on its own means 'elk'; eolhxsecg is recorded as a word for 'sedge', 'reed', or 'papyrus plant'.

"SIGEL[43] sǣmannum
symble byð on hihte,
ðonne hî hine feriað
ofer fisces bæð
oð hî brimhengest
bringeð tô lande.

Sail to seamen
is always confidence,
when they bear it
over the fishes bath,
till them the sea horse
bringeth to land.

"TIR byð tâcna sum;
healdað trywa wel
wið æðelingas:
â byð on færylde
ofer nihta genipu:
næfre swîceð.

Tir is a token;
it holdeth confidence well
with nobles:
ever is it moving
over the darkness of night:
never it resteth.

"BEORC byð blæda leâs;
bereð efne swâ ðeâh
tânas bûtan tuddre:
byð on telgum wlîtig;
byð ðeáh on helme
hyrsted fægere,
geloden leâfum,
lyfte getenge.

Birch is fruitless;
nevertheless it beareth
twigs without increase;
it is beautiful in its branches;
still it is at top
fairly adorned,
laden with leaves,
heavy in the air.

"EH byð for eorlum
æðelinga wyn,
hors hôfum wlanc
ðær him hæleðas ymb
welege on wicgum
wrixlað spræce:
and byð unstyllum
æfre frôfur.

Horse is for men
the joy of nobles,
steed proud of hoofs
where the heroes
wealthy on their horses
interchange speech:
and to the restless it is
ever a comfort.

[43] Kemble's suggestion that the 'S' rune has been treated as segel 'sail' rather than as sigel 'Sun', 'gem', has not been adopted by subsequent editors, but has much in its favour. (See Kemble's explanation on pages 34-37.)

"MAN byð on myrgðe
his magan leôf;
sceal ðeâh ânra gehwylc
ôðrum swîcan,
forðâm dryhten wile
dôme sînum
ðæt earme flǽsc
eorðan betǽcan.

Man is in mirth
dear to his kindred;
and yet must every one
depart from other,
because the Lord will
by his doom
the wretched flesh
commit to earth.

"LAGU byð leôdum
langsum geþûht,
gif hi sculun nêðan
on nacan tealtum,
and hî sǽ-ŷða
swŷðe bregað
and se brimhengest
bridles ne gŷmð.

Water to men
seemeth tedious,
if they must venture
on the unsteady boat,
and the sea waves
heavily whirl them,
and the sea stallion
heed not the bridle.

"ING wæs ǽrest
mid Eâst Denum
gesewen secgum;
oð he sîððan eft
ofer wǽg gewât
wǽn æfter ran.
Ðûs heardingas
ðone hæle nemdon

Ing was first
among the East Danes
seen by men;
till he afterwards again
departed over the wave:
his chariot ran behind him.
Thus the warriors[44]
named the man.

"EÐEL byð oferleôf
ǽghwylcum men,
gif he môt ðær rihtes
and gerysena
onbrûcan on blôde
blædum oftast.

Native land is overdear
to every man,
if he there his rights
and befitting (honour)
may enjoy in his blood
oftest with increase.

---

[44] Or Heardingas, a proper noun and tribal name.

"DÆG byð drihtnes sond,
deôre mannum,
mǽre metodes leôht,
myrgð and tôhiht
eâdgum and earmum,
eallum brice.

Day is the Lord's messenger,
dear to men,
the glorious light of God,
mirth and consolation
to rich and poor,
useful to all.

"AC byð on eorðan
elda bearnum
flǽsces fôdor,
fereð gelome
ofer ganotes bæð,
garsecg fandað,
hwæðer âc hæbbe
æðele treôw.

Oak is on earth
to the sons of men
food of the flesh,
often he goeth
over the ganets bath,
tempteth the ocean,
he that hath oak
the noble tree.[45]

"ÆSC byð oferheâh
eldum dŷre
stîð staðule
stede rihte hylt,
ðeâh him feohtan on
firas monige.

Ash is over high
dear to men,
stiff in its station
well it holdeth its place,
although against it fight
many men.

"YR byð æðelinga
and eorla gehwǽs
wyn and wyrðmynd,
byð on wicge fæger
fæstlîc on færelde,
fyrdgearewa sum.

Bow is of nobles
and of every man
joy and dignity,
it is fair on the horse,
firm in the expedition,
part of warlike arms.

[45] The last three lines of this stanza might be better translated: "ocean tests whether oak holds proper faith."

"IOR byð eafixa (sum),
and ðeâh a brûceð
fôdres on faldan,
hafað fægerne eard
wætre beworpen,
ðær he wynnum leofað.

Eel[46] (?) is a river fish,
yet ever enjoyeth
its food on the ground,
a fair dwelling hath it
surrounded with water,
where it liveth in joy.

"EAR[f] byð egle
eorla gehwylcun,
ðonn fæstlîce
flǽsc onginneð
hrâw colian,
hrusan ceôsan
blâc tô gebeddan,
bleda gedreôsað,
wynna gewîtað,
wera geswîcað.

War[47] is a terror
to every man,
when continually
the flesh beginneth
the corpse to cool,
to choose the earth
pale for its consort,
its joys depart,
its pleasures vanish,
it parteth from men.

The language, the introduction of Christian thoughts and words, and some gross blunders in the explanations given by the Anglo-Saxon poet himself, place the date of this composition at a late period. It nevertheless supplies us with valuable information. Among the most striking mistakes may be mentioned, the rendering given to Sigel. This, which in all the Teutonic tongues denotes a gem or jewel, - in a secondary sense, the sun – is here treated as if it were Segel, a sail.[g]

[46] A recent and plausable suggestion is that Ior means 'beaver' - see article in *Neuphilologische Mitteilungen* vol.81.

[f] This obscure and mythological word appears to be one of the names of Ziu, Tiw, Týr, the Old German, Anglo-Saxon, and Norse Mars. In some parts of Germany, Ertac is in use for Tuesday,(Tiwesdæg, Zistac,) and Eresberg is Mons Martis. (See, however, Grimm, Deutsche Mythologie, p. 133, 134.)

[47] Ear usually means 'ocean' in Old English; here a rarer meaning, 'earth' is implied. No subsequent editor has followed Kemble's identification of Ear with Tiw (Ares?).

[g] Were not Sigel neuter, the passage might still be construed properly; but the hî hine feriað, probably for hî him farað, renders it impossible, without correcting the text, to suppose that the writer meant anything but Segel. It is, however, to be observed that the genders are almost continually neglected in the latter lines of each stanza.

Fig. 12

Fig. 13

Fig. 14

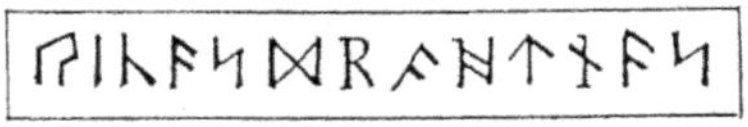

Fig. 15

Fig. 16

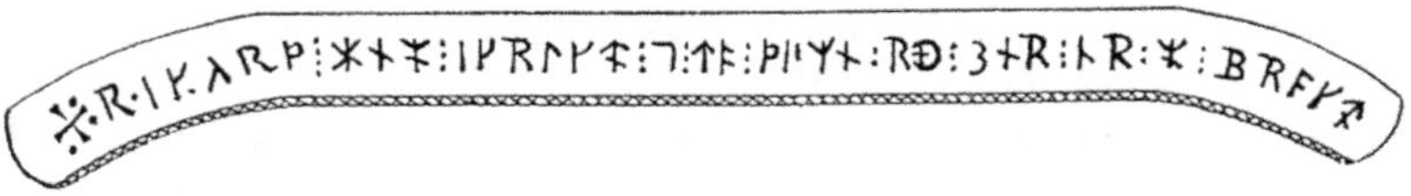

Now these, in all possible varieties which the caprice of individuals could produce, are the Anglo-Saxon, as distinguished from the Swedish, Danish, Norwegian and Icelandic Runes: and in these alone all the Anglo-Saxon inscriptions are written; even as they are all, without exception, in dialects of the Anglo-Saxon, totally free from admixture of Danish or any other tongue.

The first inscriptions I shall take are those found at the ancient Northumbrian settlement of Hartlepool. They occur on two gravestones, and have already been engraved in the Archæologia, so that it will be unnecessary to do more than give the readings of them. (Fig. 12.) these are, first,

HILDIÐRYÐ,

and second,

HILDDIGYÐ;

in which last name the second D is redundant, which led, no doubt, to the G having been afterwards cut above the line.

The next (Fig. 13.) is a stone found in Dover, and also engraved in an earlier number of the Archæologia, (XXV. p. 604), but not so successfully read as the Hartlepool inscriptions. Gisohtus, which some one suggested, was as little to be found on the stones, as it was possible for a Saxon to have borne the name. The truth is, that the seventh character is an EA, and not a T: it requires, therefore, two slight strokes at the summit of the arms. The fifth character is an L, not an O; the last but one is an R, not a U; and the last is a D, but could never have been an S. The word is ✚ GISLHEARD, which is a Saxon name.

The Bewcastle inscription (Fig. 14.) is very easy to read, and has been read with accuracy by William Grimm. At the same time it must be remembered, that the dialect of this and other inscriptions is one which at the early period when these must have been cut, made the genitive singular in *æs,* and the dative in *æ.* The words are RICÆS DRYHTNÆS,[h] [48] *domini potentis:* there has, therefore, been either a portion of the inscription lost, or the cross or pillar on which it stood was meant to be taken as part of the legend:- thus, Signum Domini Potentis.

---

[h] Rynas Dryhtnes, which some one suggested, and which has been translated *Mysteria Domini,* labours under the disadvantage of not being Anglo-Saxon.

[48] "of the powerful God".

Whether this inscription, and the stone on which it was cut, stood alone, or whether they formed part of some larger monument, I do not know. But there is at Bewcastle a pillar which is said to have been surmounted by a cross, and on which the remains - and alas! the hardly legible remains - of a long Runic inscription, may still be traced. I beg to refer to the careful copy of this, furnished by Mr. Howard, of Corby Castle, and published in the fourteenth volume of the Archæologia. This Plate (XXXIV.) contains three several portions of the inscription. Of fig.1. but one letter, an R, is now legible. Fig.2., which contains indistinct traces of nine lines of Runes, and of which the loss may be said irreparable, offers here and there a legible letter or two, but no more. Fig.3, on the contrary, is still in perfect preservation: unfortunately, it supplies us with only one word, and that a proper name - CYNIBURUG, or CYNIBURUH,[i] which contains unquestionable evidence of great antiquity. (Fig.15.) Who this lady was it would be absurd to attempt to guess; but I think that the fifth line of the inscription in fig.2 may also possibly have contained her name; while the second line of the same, commencing with letters which apparently formed the word CRIST, render it likely that this, as well as the Ruthwell pillar, was a Christian work. The most important deduction from the name I have read is, that the inscription was an Anglo-Saxon, not a Norse one.

An inscription, printed in Whitaker's History of Richmondshire, vol. ii. p.229, I shall, on this occasion, pass over. I do this on two grounds: first, because I question it being an Anglo-Saxon inscription, and still more because I have not the slightest faith in its accuracy. It is absolutely necessary that we should have a better copy of it before we can attempt to read it.

The Bridekirk inscription (Fig. 16.) is involved still in very great obscurity, owing principally to the state of dilapidation in which the font obviously is, and which, in spite of Mr. Howard's careful delineation, (Arch. vol.XIV. p. 113. and vol. XIX. p. 381.), leaves it very doubtful whether we have all the letters before us. There have been various attempts made to read the words, but none are satisfactory. Mr. Hamper's is the best, and he appears to have seized the general sense of the inscription; though   in almost every word his want of

---

[i] *Burug* and *byrug* are the usual Northumbrian forms of the West-Saxon *burh*.

accurate Anglo-Saxon betrays him into blunders. Of his reading, as well as Bishop Nicolson's, it is enough to say, that no such language ever existed as they find on this stone. In the state in which this inscription now is I cannot pretend to certainty in my exposition, particularly as many of the Runes are not in the usual Anglo-Saxon form, and several letters are altogether obliterated.

To the name RICARD I object at once: it was not in use among the Anglo-Saxons at all; and, had it been so, its form on this stone would have been RICIHARD. Further the third Rune is not the usual Anglo-Saxon C, and the last Rune is ᚦ, not D. I now suggest, whether the figure that precedes the R is so certainly a *cross*, as Mr. Howard makes it, and whether, in differing so widely as he does from older copyist, he is quite right. Without seeing the stone myself, I will not decide upon this: but I should suspect that close inquiry would furnish, in place of the cross, traces of the Runes ᚻ ᛖ or ᚻ ᚫ, viz. HE, or HÆ. I read the third Rune ᚷ G, and believe the ᚦ to be the initial of the succeeding word. The first word, then, is HERIGAR, or HÆRIGAR. Immediately after the ᚦ is a space denoted by dots, but which unquestionably was once filled with a letter: this I take to have been an I or E: the next letter is a G, the next an N, and the second word is ĐEGN. The next character, instead of being a compound rune, is a G; it is followed by an abrasion, where a portion of a Rune once stood: coupling this with the remnant of a letter still extant, it is most probable that the whole Rune was ᛖ, that is E. The next character, which was not and could not be C or G, probably has lost a slight stroke at the summit, and was a W. The next Rune but one, I take, as all my predecessors have, to be ᚩ, that is O. The next must have been an H; for it could not be a C, nor unchanged could it be a G: Mr. Hamper would have it an F, reading GEGROFT, which word he justifies by an inscription on a ring engraved in Hickes's Thesaurus. (Præf. p. xiii.) But Gegroft is not and could not be a Saxon word; the verb gegrafan, to engrave, making its preterite gegrôf, and it being utterly impossible for a T to be appended to any such preterite.[k] The final T, not TE, is admitted; and I believe the dots which follow it, coupled with the strokes that remain, to have been an ᛖ, that is E. The third word then would be GEWROHTE. The

[k] The reading of the inscription in Hickes is as follows: ✚ Aeðred mec ah. Eanred mec agrof. ✚ That is, Æðred owns me, Eanred carved me.

next word must be a mere guess, the first and last letters being now obliterated: it is possible that it may have been ᚢ ᛏ ᚫ ᛚ, UTÆL, a name of frequent occurrence among the signatures of Anglo-Saxon charters. The next letter is clearly a ᚦ then follow the fragments of what seems to have been an, E; G and N are plain, and we again have the word ÐEGN. The next word is also merely made up of guesses; it being obvious that this part of the inscription is hopelessly abraded. The first letter I suppose to have been an I; the next is an R: the third, which varies much in the several copies, seems to have been an ill formed ᛗ, M; I venture to guess that the next was an U: N and R are plain: the dots probably once made an I: K is plain. The next which looks like an R, might still easily be an Y: the dots I take to have represented an S:- the word so guessed at is IRMUNRICYS. Supplying the E, which is wanting in the second place of the next word, we have GEBROHT, or, as it may be, GEBROHTÆ; and the whole inscription will be

HERIGAR ÐEGN GEWROHTE.UTÆL ÐEGN IRMUNRICYS GEBROHTE

This interpretation, I fairly confess, is anything but satisfactory to myself: all that it can claim for itself is, that it is Anglo-Saxon, which no other explanation hitherto published, is. The meaning is,

"Heregar the Thane wrought it.
Utel, Eormanric's Thane, brought it."

I now proceed to an inscription which has long been considered as hopeless, and which no doubt is very difficult. But the difficulties arise merely from the dilapidated state of the stone, by which large portions of the writing have been lost: what remains entire is as easy to read as any inscription can be expected to be. I allude to the Cross at Ruthwell, on the Scottish Border. This noble monument, which has been rescued by the Rev. Mr. Duncan from the further ravages of neglect, has been several times described, with more or less accuracy. I use the copy of the inscription given by Hickes in his Thes. Gram. Isl. Tab. IIII.; by Gordon in his Itinerarium Septentrionale, p. 160; and lastly the accurate and beautiful delineation furnished by Mr. Duncan to the Society of Antiquaries of Scotland, and engraved for their Archæologia, 1834, Pt II.

It is a lamentable thing that no early copy should have been made of this before the sacrilegious fury of the Presbyterian iconoclasts, in 1642, caused the Cross to be flung down, and deprived us, probably for ever, of the hope of supplying the missing portion of the inscription. But it is also very strange that none of our philologists and antiquaries have so much as attempted to give anything like a reasonable account of the few lines we have: that Hickes should have shrugged his shoulders at them, and William Grimm shaken his head, and passed on. Two learned Icelanders, however, with great valour, if not much discretion, have appeared in the field, to shame both England and Germany; Finn Magnusen in Copenhagen, and Repp in Edinburgh, have thrown down the gauntlet to the degenerate antiquaries of England; with what success we shall see hereafter. The plate of the Ruthwell Cross (Fig. 17.) requires some little explanation. III. is one of the two corresponding broad faces of a the pillar; I. and II. on the contrary, are the sides, which are not quite so broad as the faces. The broader faces are sculptured with various scriptural subjects, in compartments; and on the spaces which separate one relief from the other, are inscriptions in Latin characters, referring to the subject matter of each compartment. These inscriptions begin, over the head of the figure, to the left, descend along the right side, and then return to the top of the left side. The centre figure on each side appears to be the principal one, and is rather the largest. One of these represents Christ glorified and trampling on the fiends, represented by swine; the other depicts Mary Magdalene washing the feet of the Saviour. Round the latter is the inscription ✠ ATTVLIT ALABASTRVM VNGVENTI ET STANS RETROSECVS PEDES EIVS LACRIMIS COEPIT RIGARE PEDES EIVS ET CAPILLIS CAPITIS SVI TERGEBAT.[49] The corresponding inscription on the other side is as follows: ✠ IHS. XPS IVDEX AEQVITATIS SERTO SALVATOREM MVNDI BESTIAE ET DRACONES COGNOVERVNT INDE.[50]

The two sides of the cross have also their sculpture and inscriptions. The former reaches unbroken up to the level of the top of the principal compartment on the broad faces: the continuation of it above this seems to have been an after thought, as the arabesques are interrupted by the raised edge, and the execution of the upper portion is said to be inferior.

---

[49] "She brought a jar of ointment and standing close up to his feet began to wash his feet with her tears and dried them with the hair of her head." From Luke 7.37-8

[50] Kembles version is incomplete; the inscription in fact reads: ✠ IHS XPS IUDEX. AEQUITATIS. BESTIAE. ET. DRACONES. COGNOVERUNT. IN. DES. ERTO. SALVATOREM. MUNDI. ✠ - that is, "Jesus Christ, Judge of Even-handedness; the beasts and dragons acknowledged, in the desert, the Saviour of the world." This is not a Biblical quotation, but reflects texts like Psalm 91.13, Psalm 96.10, Psalm 148. 7, 10, Psalm 104, Isaiah 43.20, Acts 17.31.

It is along the raised edge of the sides that the Runic inscription is cut, which we are now to investigate; a matter which would hardly have presented any difficulty had the lower part of the stone not been defaced, and so the connecting lines of the inscription obliterated. And what then is the meaning and object of this Runic inscription? Repp says it records the grant of a font, which he calls a Christ-bason (!) and of some cows and lands in Ashlafardhal, a place that never existed, by the advice of the Monks or Fathers of Therfuse, a monastery of which no one ever heard. Professor Finn Magnusen improves on his learned countryman - makes the cross out to be the record of Ashlof's marriage settlements, gives us chapter and verse for Ashlof, with a full account of her birth, parentage and education, and winds up 105 stupendous pages, by composing a chapter of Anglo-Saxon history, such as I will take it upon myself to say was never ventured before by the wildest dreamer even in Denmark. I should not be doing the learned Professor justice, if I did not quote his translation at full length. Here it is;- "I, Offa Woden's kinsman, transfer to Eska's descendant, to you two the property, field, meadow, give we Ashlof! The words of the noble I below make known. To Erinc young promised *she* riches, estates good; I for the *marriage* feast prepare in the mean time. Received he now, - the noble spoke, - the gift, and aye preside in the hall *over* the guests! I have magnanimity, I bring rings . . . . These three estates Erincred possesses. Christ was among...... when to all we gave all that they owned - the married pair: At their home, the rich women's, you were a guest, *their* down dwelling - - - Give every ..... the advice is willing (willingly given). Back spoliation, if *yet living* on earth! Well the Ætheling possesses now me this property. Saw I us my Son! Every where again rule!" The italics are, no doubt, put in to show the scrupulous accuracy with which the translation has been made; and by their help it seems to run on all fours: unluckily there is not one word of it on the pillar.

Duncan (D)

Fig. 17

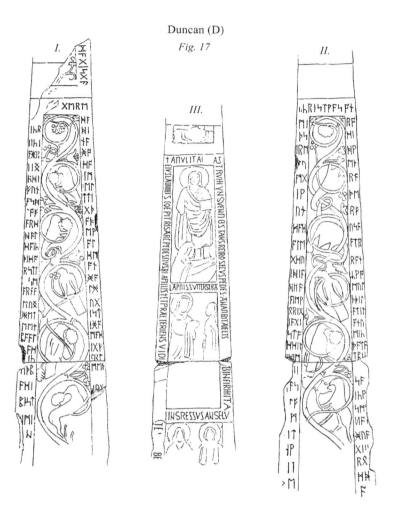

Now it is very remarkable, that both Repp and Magnusen have read the mere letters with tolerable accuracy: it is only when they come to divide them into words, that their good star deserts them. This can arise from nothing but their Danish prepossessions and imperfect acquaintance with Anglo-Saxon and its northern dialects. Hence Repp amuses himself with jumbling Dansk and Anglo-Saxon together; one word of one language, one word of another, just as may best make out his story of the Christ bason: while Magnusen plumes his wings for a high flight; and, having invented an Offa, Erincred and Eska, a history and a wedding, completes his large plan by inventing a new language, in which he says the inscription is written, and a people, by whom he says the language was spoken.

The inscription is in the usual Anglo-Saxon Runes, in that Anglo-Saxon dialect which was spoken in Northumberland in the eighth and ninth centuries, and the fragments of it which remain contain a few couplets of a religious poem relating to the events represented in the two principle compartments, viz. the washing the Saviour's feet by Mary Magdalene, and the glorification of Christ through his passion. Having said thus much of its general meaning, I proceed to illustrate it more in detail; and I only regret that the want of a fount of Anglo-Saxon Runes prevents me placing the letters side by side. I shall, however, follow the tables seriatim, using Hickes's, Gordon's, or Duncan's readings, in proportion as one seems more accurate than the other.

Fig. I. - On the right-hand margin of the compartment, above the horizontal line, in a different position from all the rest of the inscription, stand the letters D (or M) ÆGISGÆ.[m] On the transverse rim across the shaft stand the four Runes, GERE.

For convenience of reference, I have given copies of the inscriptions according to Hickes and Gordon. Figs 18 and 19.

I. 1.1. Previous to these characters, which are placed two lines lower than the transverse margin, Hickes and Gordon place the fragments of letters now illegible. I shall assume by and by, that the last of these was an M. 1.3. Duncan gives a very ill-informed and doubtful R, Hickes a

---

[m] These letters have been left entirely out of consideration, partly because it is very questionable whether they formed part of the original inscription: but still more because, from the ruined state of the stone, their connexion with any other Runes is now impossible to be made out.

distinct one, as the last letter. Gordon reads U: there can be no question but that it is a Y. 1.5. Hickes reads the last letter as T; Duncan and Gordon have I, which is right. 1.8. The initial L, wanting in Duncan, is very clear in the other two copies. The second letter, doubtful in Gordon, and rather O than A in Duncan, is certainly A in Hickes. 1.9. A in Hickes, doubtful in Gordon, but probably also A; Æ in Duncan. 1.12. NI clear in Hickes and Duncan, in Gordon only two strokes. 1.13. Æ clear in Hickes and Gordon, abraded in Duncan. 1.14. BI very distinct in Hickes and Gordon, wanting altogether in Duncan. 1.15. ÆD clear in Hickes, the last letter doubtful in Gordon, the two last in Duncan. 1.16. E doubtful in Gordon, but very clear in Duncan; in Hickes the whole line omitted. 1.19. in Gordon the three last letters doubtful; in Duncan the last is rather L than T, which Hickes reads rightly. 1.20. Gordon reads the first letter clearly: Hickes and Duncan omit it. 1.21. Gordon and Hickes have the first letter which Duncan omits. 1.22. The rest is found only in Duncan.

II. 1.4. Hickes GA, Gordon and Duncan rather GO. 1.5. Æ Gordon, A Hickes and Duncan. 1.7. The last letter in Hickes and Gordon and Duncan resembles an L; it probably has lost the lower stroke, and should read Æ. 1.8. The first letter is clearly a T in Hickes, but is very confused in Gordon and Duncan: I suggest an S. 1.10. The last letter doubtful in Duncan, but very clear in Gordon and Hickes.1.14. A clear in Duncan and Hickes, doubtful in Gordon. 1.20. The second letter A in Duncan, Æ in Hickes, O in Gordon. 1.22. nearly lost in Duncan, ÆRE in Hickes, ORE in Gordon. 1.23, only in Duncan.

The Ruthwell Cross

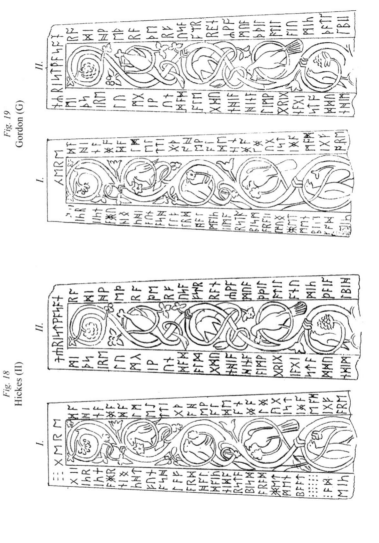

Fig. 18
Hickes (II)

Fig. 19
Gordon (G)

44

I.		II.	
1.	IKR	1.	DÆ
2.	IIKN	2.	HI
3.	ÆKR	3.	NÆ
4.	NING	4.	GA
5.	KHI	5.	MÆ
6.	FUN	6.	LD
7.	ÆSH	7.	EL
8.	LAF	8.	TTI
9.	ARD	9.	GTH
10.	HÆL	10.	AH
11.	DAIK	11.	EW
12.	NIDA	12.	AL
13.	RSTÆ	13.	DE
14.	BISM	14.	AN
15.	ÆRED	15.	GA
16.	EUNG	16.	LG
17.	KET	17.	UG
18.	MEN	18.	IST
19.	BAÆT	19.	IGA
20.	GÆD	20.	MOD
21.	ɬ IK	21.	IGF
22.	ɫITHB	22.	ORE
23.	ÆDI	23.	MEN
24.	BIST		
25.	ɬMI		
26.	ɪɛH		

The letters above the transverse line, I leave out of the question altogether, believing them to have nothing to do with the rest of the inscription; to be very probably a latter addition; and even if not so, to be now so isolated from their context as to be unintelligible. The first line on the left I read thus:

....MIK. RIIKNÆ KYNINGK. HIFUNÆS HLAFARD. HÆLDA IK NI DARSTÆ. BISMÆREDE UNGKET MEN. BA ÆT GÆD(R)E. IK(N)IÐ BÆDI BIST(E)ME(D): that is,

....me. The Powerful King, the Lord of Heaven, I dared not hold. They reviled us two, both together. I stained with the pledge of crime .....

Now commencing with the transverse line, and continuing down the right hand column, the words run thus:

GEREDÆ HINÆ. GAMÆLDÆ. ESTIG ÐA HE WALDE. AN GALGU GISTIGA. MODIG FORE MEN.......: that is,

prepared himself: he spake benignantly when he would go up upon the cross, courageously before men......

Proceeding now to the other side of the cross, and taking first the left hand column, next the transverse rim ✠ CIST WÆS ON, and then the right hand column, we have the following letters:

Left hand margin		Right hand margin	
1.	MI	1.	RO
2.	THS	2.	DI
3.	IRE	3.	HW
4.	LU	4.	ETH
5.	MG	5.	RÆ
6.	IW	6.	THE ⚏
7.	UN	7.	RF
8.	DÆD	8.	USÆ
9.	ALE	9.	FEAR
10.	GDU	10.	RAN
11.	NHLÆ	11.	CWO
12.	HINÆ	12.	MU ⚏ Æ
13.	LIMW	13.	THTHIL
14.	ORIG	14.	ÆTIL
15.	NÆGI	15.	ANU
16.	STO	16.	MIC
17.	DDU	17.	THÆTA
18.	NHIM	18.	LB⚏IH
19.	⚏	19.	⚏
20.	⚏ ÆS	20.	SÆ
21.	⚏LF	21.	IKW⚏
22.	⚏ D	22.	SM⚏
23.	⚏ T	23.	GA⚏
24.	⚏W	24.	GUÆ
25.	⚏	25.	G⚏
26.	⚏E	26.	RO
		27.	DH
		28.	A

46

I. 1.3. All the copies read IRE. I believe a cross stroke over the I to have been lost, and read TRE. 1.4. The L, which is partly abraded in Duncan, is clear in Gordon and Hickes. 1.8. A in Duncan, Æ in Gordon and Hickes. 1.9. Æ in Hickes, A in Gordon and Duncan. 1.13. ÆIM in Hickes, LIM in Gordon and Duncan. 1.14. O in Gordon and Duncan, G in Hickes. 1.15. Duncan and Hickes read the first letter I, Gordon distinctly N which I prefer, on palæographical grounds: the word makes equally good sense whether we take it to be the nom. pl. which would be the case with Duncan's reading, or the acc. sing. with Gordon's. 1.20. and the rest only in Duncan, and very mutilated.

II. Transverse line. The cross before the words is indistinct in Duncan. 1.12. The last letter, which in Hickes and Gordon is distinctly Æ, has lost the lower stroke in Duncan, and appears like an L. 1.15. Duncan and Gordon clearly an A; Hickes perhaps an Æ. The second letter clear in Duncan and Hickes; doubtful in Gordon. 1.17. The second letter distinctly Æ in Hickes and Gordon, but A in Duncan; the third letter doubtful in Hickes, clear in Gordon and Duncan. 1.18. The first letter is perfectly distinct in Hickes and Gordon, but doubtful in Duncan. From 1.19. is found only in Duncan, and from the state of dilapidation of the stone, can only be guessed at. The inscription then I read thus;

I. MITH STRELUM GIWUNDÆD. ALEGDUN HIÆ HINÆ. LIM-WERIGNÆ. GISTODDUN HIM........

wounded with shafts. They laid him down, limb-weary. They stood by him.......

II. ✚ KRIST WÆS ON RODI. HWETHRÆ TI LÆNUM. IK THÆT AL BIH.......SÆ IK W(Æ)S MI(D) GA(L)GU Æ(.........)ROD. HA..............

Christ was on the cross. Lo! There with speed, came from afar nobles to him in misery. I that all beh(eld ....) I was with the cross ....

Before I leave this noble monument of Anglo-Saxon antiquity, I shall take the liberty of making a few philological remarks on the versification and language, the latter of which is in fact the strongest proof of the accuracy of my reading. We have proportions of four columns of verse, which must be thus arranged:

......mik.	.....geredæ	....	+ Krist wæs on
Riikne kyningk	hinæ gamældæ	mid strelum gi-	rôdi
hifunæs hlafard	estig ða he walde	wundæd	hweðræ ther fûsæ
hælda ik ni darstæ	an galgu gistîga	alegdun hiæ hinæ	fearran cwomu
bismærede ungket	môdig fore	limwêrigne	æððilæ ti lænum
men	men	gistôddun him ..	ic that al bih(eôld)
bâ ætgæd(r)e	....	....	......sæ(...)
ik (n)iðbædi bist-	....	....	ic w(æ)s mi(d)
(e)me(d)	....	....	ga(l)gu
....	....	....	æ(...)rod . ha ..
....			....
....			

Fragmentary as these lines are, the alliteration[51] is perfectly obvious in the first, third, and fourth columns. The second has none in the third and fourth lines, which is sufficient grounds for believing that the suggestion ESTIG is not altogether accurate; it requires a word commencing with G: but I could not suggest one that would not do violence to the traces of letters which remain, beyond the fair liberty of interpretation. The dialect of these lines is that of Northumberland in the seventh, eighth, and even ninth centuries, and from the mass of Northumbrian documents which we possess is capable of easy comparison. The first characteristic peculiarity is the *æ* for *e* in the oblique cases, and which I have observed in the contemporaneous MS. of Cuðberht's letter, at St. Gallen, from which, as a singular and noble monument of language, I cite the words quoted by the dying Beda:

Fore the neidfaerae	Before the necessary journey
naenig uuiurthit	no one is
thonc-snotturra	wiser of thought
than him tharf sie	than he hath need,
to ymbhycgannae	to consider
aer his hiniongae	before his departure,
huaet his gastae	what for his spirit
godaes aeththa yflaes	of good or evil
æfter deothdaege	after the death-day
doemid uuieorthae.	shall be doomed.

[51] While correctly identifying the Ruthwell Cross inscription as poetry, Kemble does not seem at first to have made the connection with the Old English poem *The Dream of the Rood*, which the inscription closely parallels: see text in *Sweet's Reader* ed. Whitelock, or Swanton's edition of *The Dream of the Rood* (1969): Kemble did however make this connection later (in *Archaeologia* vol.30, 1844).

This, which is strictly organical, and represents the uncorrupted Gothic Genitive in *as* and dative in *a*, as well as the Old Saxon forms of the substantive, is evidence of great antiquity: it was one of the first forms that perished as the language became what is somewhat questionably called improved and polished. Till the middle of the ninth century this is found in Northumberland and Kent: and so also the *a* for the usual West-Saxon *o*, in Hlafard, generally Hlâford, but which here in col.1. has the archaic form. But that which is perhaps the most characteristic of the Northumbrian dialect is the formation of the infinitive in *a* or *æ*, instead of *an*. We have two instances of this, namely hælda in the first and gistiga in the second column: but this, which is essential to the dialect, and in which it resembles the old Norse and Frisic, is so sure a test that it is enough of itself to decide upon the true locality of any inscription or manuscript.[n] The Durham book (MS. Cott. Nero, D. iv.) has I believe throughout but one single verb which makes its infinitive in *an*, and that is the anomalous verb bian, *to be*, even wosa and wiortha following the common rule. I subjoin a few examples:

geboeta *emendasse.* gebrenga *traducere.* geceasa *captari.* unclænsia *inquinare.* geceyga *vocare.* gecoma, gecumae, gecyma *venire.* gecuoeða *dicere.* gedoema *arbitrari.* gedoa *facere.* druncnia *mergi.* fordoa *perdere.* gedeigla *abscondi.* æteaua *ostendere.* eatta *manducare.* oferfara *transire.* ondfoa *accipere.* geflitta *contendere.* gegema *corrigere.* forgeafa *ignosci.* gehera *servire.* huerfa *mutuari.* gehera *audire.* gehyda *abscondi.* habba *habere.* geleda *traducere.* eftarisa *resurgere.* astiga *ascendere.* spreca *loqui.* sealla *dare.* gesea *videre.* onsaca *abnegari.* wiðsaca *repelli.* gespreca *loqui.* sueria *jurare.* efttotea *retrahere.* gewuna *manere.* wutta *nosce.* wosa *esse.* weortha *esse.* gewyrca *facere.* gewiga *postulare.* gewrixla *mutare.* ðerhwunia *perseverare.* geþenca *cogitare.* geþolega *pati.*

[n] This has been attributed to Danish influence, because about the beginning of the ninth century the Danes began to ravage Northumberland. To this I answer, that it is universal in the Northumbrian monuments anterior to the Danish invasion. For its Frisic origin much more may be said; but it is generally forgotten that Procopius names the Frisians among the earliest Teutonic colonists of Britain. Throughout this paper I beg to observe that I use *Northumbrian* in the Anglo-Saxon, and not the English, meaning of the word.

The Durham Ritual, now in course of publication by the Surtees Club, contains equally strong evidence of the real form of the Northumbrian infinitive.

The word Hifunæs differs from the usual Anglo-Saxon form Heofones; but the variation is a proof only of antiquity. The Gothic word Sibuns, *seven*, in like manner became first Sifun, then Seofon or Seofen. Just so here, the Gothic word Hibuns, which once existed, first became Hifun, afterwards Heofon and Heofen.

The word Ungket is another incontrovertible proof of extreme antiquity; having to the best of my knowledge never been found but in this passage. It is the dual accusative of the first pronoun personal Ic, and corresponds to the very rare dual of the second personal pronoun, Incit, which occurs twice in Cædmon, p. 165 and p. 174, and from which James Grimm long ago predicted the appearance of this *uncit*, at some other time or other. (Deut. Gramm. I. p. 781.)

Walde, in column 2, is the Northumbrian form of the more usual *wôlde,* I would. It is of universal occurrence in the Durham Evangeles and the other Northumbrian documents, as well as the negative Nalde, I *would not*, more commonly *nôlde.*

The termination -un for -on is further evidence of antiquity, and, though not by any means confined to Northumberland, was of constant use there.

The only word that remains to be noticed is Fearran, in col 4, instead of the more usual *feorran*. This, however, is no inaccuracy, but the common Northumbrian form, continually occurring in the Durham Evangeles and Ritual. Cwomu for Cwomun in the same line can only be looked upon as a piece of carelessness, since the stone shews no sign of abrasion here, and no dialect of Anglo-Saxon could omit this final N.[52] The Norse did indeed omit it, but I beg once and for all to say that Norse forms have nothing whatever to do with Anglo-Saxon inscriptions. It was by trusting to Norse forms that Thorkelin misread every line and mistranslated nearly every word of Beôwulf. It is by trusting to Norse forms that Dr. Repp has plunged himself into his ludicrous *Christ-bason,* and that Finn Magnusen has recorded his own rashness throughout 105 of the most adventurous pages I ever

---

[52] But see Campbell *Old English Grammar* para. 472. This does not affect an eighth century date for the Ruthwell Cross, however.

remember to have read. One word more: this, like every other Anglo-Saxon composition is as strict in its grammar and its grammatical forms as any passage from any Greek or Latin classic: and in construing such compositions just as little can be left to chance as we leave to chance in rendering sentences from Thucydides or Cicero.

I shall not attempt now to investigate any other inscriptions, as I am not aware of there being any which are written in Anglo-Saxon: and I therefore hasten to say a few words of the use of runes in manuscripts. This is confined for the most part to MSS. of late date, and periods when paganism had long ceased to be connected with this alphabet. The first and simplest use of them is where they serve the purpose of a kind of short-hand, the figure of the rune being written instead of the word which was its name. Thus the priest who wrote the interlinear glosses to the Rushworth Book, now in the Bodleian Library, meaning to write *Færman* Presbyter þas boc gloesede,[53] uses the Runic M (MAN) instead of the last three letters of his name. So again in Beôwulf (ll 1035. 1819.)[54] we twice find the rune Eðel instead of the word, apparently introduced for no purpose on earth but to save the transcriber the trouble of writing the word at length. And so in the Durham Rituals the words *dæg* and *man* are, almost without exception, replaced by the Runes bearing those names. There are two passages in Anglo-Saxon poems which introduce several such characters in this way, but with a definite object, to which I will call attention. In the Vercelli MS. is contained a long poem on the finding of the cross by the Empress Helena: after the close of the poem, and apparently intended as a tail-piece to the whole book, comes a poetical passage consisting of one hundred and sixty lines, in which the author principally refers to himself, and after a reference to his own increasing age and the change from the strength and joyousness of youth, he breaks out into moralizing strain, in which he concludes his work. The following lines, containing Runes, form a portion of this poem.

[53] "Færman the priest glossed this book."

[54] In modern numeration, lines 520, 913; the Rune also occurs in line 1702.

A wæs sæc oð ðæt	Ever till then was the man
cynssed cearwelmum,	tossed with the waves of care,
ᚲ . drûsende,	the bold one, sinking,
ðeâh he in medohealle	though in the meadhall he
mâðmas þege,	received treasures,
æplede gold;	dappled gold;
ᛗ. gnornode,	he lamented his misery,
ᛉ . gefera	the enforced comrade
nearusorge dreâh,	suffered close sorrow,
enge rûne,	a narrow mystery,
ðær him ᛗ . fore	when the steed before him
milpaðas mæt,	measured the mile paths,
môdig þrægde,	boldly hastened,
wîrum gewlenced.	adorned with wires.
ᚹ . is geswîðrad	Hope is violated
gomen æfter gearum,	pleasure after years,
geôgoð is gecyrred,	youth is departed,
ald onmedla:	his ancient pride:
ᚻ . wæs geara	of old* it was
geôgoðhâdes gleâm,	the exultation of youth,
nû synt geardagas	now are the days of life
æfter fyrstmearce	after the appointed time
forðgewitene,	departed,
lifwynne geliden,	life-joys slid away,
swâ. ᚱ . tôglîdeð,	as water glideth,
flôdas gefŷsde.	floods hastened.
ᚠ . æghwâm bið	Money is to every one
læne under lyfte.	mean under the heaven,
landes frætwa	the ornaments of the land
gewîtað under wolcnum, etc.	depart under the welkin, etc.[55]

The extreme rudeness and abruptness of these lines and the apparent uselessness of the Runes, led me to suspect that there was more in them than merely met the eye. And this I found to be the case: for on taking the Runes out of context, using them as single letters and uniting them

---

* See footnote 57

[55] The poetry quoted is *Elene* lines 1256-1271

in one word, they supplied me with the name CYNEWULF, undoubtedly none other than the author of the poems. It was now with the utmost interest that I read the following passage from the still more celebrated Codex Exoniensis, fol. 19, b.

ðær monig beôð	There shall many be
on gemôt læded,	led into the meeting,
fore onsyne	before the face
êces dêman.	of the Eternal Judge.
Ðonne ú cwacað; gehŷrað	Then shall the bold quake; shall hear
cyning mæðlan,	the king discourse,
rodera ryhtend sprecan	the Ruler of the Heavens speak
rêðe word ðâm ðe him	stern words to them who him
ǽr in worulde	before that in the world
wâce hŷrdon,	weakly (ill) obeyed,
þendan ᛗ 7 ᚾ	while misery and need
ŷðast meahtan	might most easily
frôfre findan.	find consolation.
Ðær sceal forht monig	There shall many a one in terror
on ðâm wongstede	on that plain
wêrig bîdan,	weary wait,
hwæt him æfter dædum	what to him after his deeds
dêman wille	(God) shall adjudge
wrâðra wîta.	of angry penalties.
bið se ᚹ scæcen,	Hope hath departed,
eorðan frætwa;	the treasures of earth;
ᚻ wæs longe	long was it of old
ᚠ flôdum bilocen,	surrounded with the sea-streams,[p]
lifwynna dǽl,	a portion of the joy of life,
ᚠ on foldan;	money on the earth;
ðonne frætwe sculon	then shall treasures
byrnan on bæle, &c.	burn in fire, etc.[56]

Here then we have the same Runes, and that in a passage which bears a remarkable similarity in the thoughts and images to the one last cited: only the Rune ᛗ i.e. E, is wanting, from which we may conclude that

---

[p] The Anglo-Saxons believed the world to be inclosed within four (or two seas), fresh and salt: hence the constantly recurring phrase, be sæm tweonum, etc etc.

[56] The poetry quoted is *Christ* lines 795-808.

53

at least one couplet is lost. I cannot here bestow space upon a long argument to show who this Cynewulf[57] was: I believe him to have been the Abbot of Peterborough of that name, who flourished in the beginning of the eleventh century, who was accounted in his own day a celebrated poet, both in Latin and Anglo-Saxon, whose works have long been reputed lost, but whose childish ingenuity has now enabled us with some probability to assign to him the authorship of the Vercelli and Exeter Codices.

It is more to my purpose to show how the use of the Runes has degenerated. I have twice rendered Cên, by "the bold": now this strictly speaking could not be done: for in the first place the adjective answering to our word *keen* is not *cên* but *cênë*: and in the next place, cên denotes *a torch*, as is apparent not only from the context in the Rune poem, but from the old German Glosses, Kero. 126. fax, fachla edo, *ken.* Paris Glosses, fax: facla, *chen.* (Diutiska. I. 225.) In this case then it is clear that some license was taken by the poet, and that, if the word was one very nearly resembling the name of the Rune, he thought himself at liberty to use this, although in a sense which the name of the Rune really never bore. In the same way in the Exeter Book the Rune Wên, which properly denotes *hope,* is used for the word of the same sound, but different spelling, denoting a waggon (wæn. N. E. wain). And so in the two passages now under consideration Ur, which strictly signifies the Urus or Bull bison of the German forests, is merely used for the same sounding word ûr (of old).

Not content with having once already given us this acrostic of his name, the poet repeats it at a later period in the Exeter book, and in a manner which renders it very difficult to translate the lines, so great is their obscurity.

[57] Sisam's *Studies in the History of Old English Literature* (1953) conclude, from the form of the name in the poems, that Cynewulf belonged to the 9th century. In the passage from *Elene*, Sisam prefers yfel "evil" or ûre "our" for the expansion of the 'U' Rune, to Kemble's "of old".

Đonne me gedælað	Then for me shall part
deôrast ealra,	the dearest of all,
sibbe tôslîtað	their relationship shall sever
sinhiwan tu,	the two consorts,
micle môdlufan;	their great love;
mîn sceal of lîce	then shall from the body
sâwul on sîðfæt,	my soul upon its journey,
nât ic sylfa hwider,	I know not myself whither,
eardes uncyððu,	what unknown land,
of sceal ic þissum	I must from this
sêcan ôðerne,	another dwelling seek,
ǽrgewyrhtum,	according to my old doings,
gongan iudædum.	go according to my ancient deeds.
Geômor hweorfeð	Sadly will wander
ᛣ . ᛙ. 7. ᚾ.	C, Y and N,
cyning bið rêðe,	stern will be the king,
sigora syllend,	the giver of glory,
ðonne synnum fâh	then stained with sins
. ᛗ . ᛈ . 7. ᚢ .	E, W and U
acle bîdað,	in terror will abide,
hwæt him æfter dǽdum	what to them after their deeds
dêman wille	he will doom
lifes tô leâne.	as retribution for their life.
ᛚ . ᚠ . beofað,	L, F will tremble,
seômað sorgcearig,	sorrowful they will lour,
synna wunde;	with the wounds of sins;
sâr eal gemon	the pain I shall all remember
ðe ic sîð oððe ǽr	which I before or since
geworhte in worulde,	wrought in the world,
ðæt ic wôpig sceal	that shall I with weeping,
tearum mǽnan.	moan with tears.[58]

It is evident that the poet literally means to use the letters that make up his name, and that he does not introduce them as words, which he had done in the passage previously quoted.

[58] The poetry quoted is *Juliana* lines 697-712.

This riddling use of the Runes brings us to a common practice in the Exeter Book: it is well known that many pages of that collection are filled with ænigmas. Now some of these are rendered even more obscure by the introduction of these characters. Many of these I must confess remain unexplained; but with one or two I have been more successful, and it may not be uninteresting to give the explanation of what our simple-minded forefathers may have exercised their wits upon, ten centuries ago.

The first of these riddles is engraved by Hickes, Thes. Gr. Ist. Tab. VI.

Ic seâh ᛋ ᚱ ᚠ ᚻ	I saw a SROH (horse),
hygewloncne	proud of spirit,
heâfodbeorhtne,	bright of head,
swiftne ofer sælwong	swift over the level plain
swîðe þrægan;	strongly run;
hæfde him on hrycge	he had upon his back
hildeþrŷðe ᚾ ᚠ ᛗ,	a NOM (man) bold in war,
nægledne râd.	a studded saddle.
ᚠ ᚾ ᛗ ᚹ wîdlast	The wide wandering ANEW (waggoner)
ferede ryne,	bore in his course,
strong on râde,	strong in his saddle,
rôfne ᛚ ᚠ ᚠ ᚠ ᚻ	a proud KOFOAH (hawk);
fôr wæs ðŷ beorhtre	the brighter was the passage
swylcra sîðfæt.	the journey of such.
Saga hwæt ic hâtte.	Say what is my name![59]

The second which is of the same kind, occurs also in the same book.

Ic swîftne geseâh	I beheld swift
on swaðe feran	on the swathe to go
ᚻ ᚾ ᚾ ᚻ ic âne geseah	a DNUH (hound): alone I saw
idese sittan.	a lady sit.[60]

[59] The poem quoted is the Exeter Book *Riddle 19*, which seems to have no answer, as it asks no particular question.

[60] The second poem quoted is the Exeter Book *Riddle 75/76*. The passage is thought to contain two riddles, possibly fragments: the first ends with its solution: HUND.

I will not venture to say what may be the meaning attempted to be conveyed in either of these riddles, although my present impression is that both contain mythological allusions. But the Runes in them made them riddles to the eye as well as the ear, and till the meaning of the Cabalistical characters themselves was ascertained, it was hopeless to attempt the solution of the difficulty. This was increased in these cases by the Runic words being written backwards, that is from right to left. Thus in the first line of the first riddle SROH for HORS, afterwards NOM for MON, ANEW for WENA, and KOFOAH for HAOFOK: and in the second, DNUH for HUND.[r]

The practice of writing the name of the person who had composed or transcribed a book, in Runic characters, is not uncommon either at home or abroad. The length to which this paper has already extended forbids my wasting time and space upon so intrinsically unimportant a portion of my subject: but it may be worth while to give the reading of a few of these colophons.

No.1. Is in Runes of a rather unusual and fantastic kind: they are German characters, differing slightly from those of the Nordalbingians and Anglo-Saxons: when deciphered, they give the following Latin lines:

OMNIS LABOR FINEM HABET PREMIUM EIUS NON HABET FINEM MADALFRID SCRIPTSIT ISTAM PARTEM DO GRATIAS QUOD PERFECI OPUS MEUM.[61]

These figures, which were communicated to Aufsesse. Anzeige for 1834, from a MS. at Freisingen, No. iv 6, b. by Professor Massmann, are supposed to be of the ninth century, an antiquity which I greatly doubt. The practised reader will perceive at once that some of the old and well-known runes appear here under new, unusual, and rather ornamented forms. (Fig. 20.)

---

[r] Professor Finn Magnusen, in an essay on the Runic Inscriptions at Blekingen, states that those Runes also are to be read from right to left. This may be: but I do not at all subscribe to the professor's readings, which appear to me to rest solely on a total misconception of a passage in Saxo Grammaticus. This, their proper business, I leave to the antiquaries of Denmark.

[61] "Every task has an end. Its reward (though) has no end. M. wrote this section. (I give) thanks to God [DO, not DO] that I have completed my work."

No.2. From the Harl. MS. 1772, containing a very early copy of the Latin Bible, written in Germany, I take the following notice in large and beautifully executed Runes (Fig. 21.) The characters in the original are nearly three quarters of an inch high.

EGO IUSUES HACSI INDIGNUS DIACON ANC LIBRUM QUEM AD OPUS PECULIARE UOLO OFF SCO.[62]

No.3. William Grimm, in his book Ueber Deutsche Runen, gives a similar entry in Anglo-Saxon Runes from a MS. at Strasbourg (Fig. 22): when read, this gives us the name ERCÆNFRIT, where the last letter, T for TH, betrays a German rather than an English hand.

No.4. Is from a MS. of Aldhelm de Virginitate in the Library of Corpus Christi College, Cambridge. (Fig. 23.) It contains the name of the lady who transcribed the book; I read it thus: ÆÐILFLÆD DESCRIPSIT.[63]

There are several other Runic lines, some printed in Hickes, some in my own collection, which can hardly be looked upon as anything but the idle amusement of transcribers, (See fig. 24) some of them being apparently mere collections of consonants without vowels, and vowels without consonants.[s]

[62] "I, I.H., unworthy deacon, wish to offer this book which (is) special [or privately owned?] work to the saint." Derolez reads Iusueus not Iusues.

[63] "Æðilflæd wrote it out."

[s] There are inscriptions in Anglo-Saxon Runes, but in no Teutonic language. The Runic legend on two rings, mentioned in the twenty-first volume of the Archæologia, are certainly not in Anglo-Saxon or any cognate tongue. Rask supposed them to be Celtic, a conclusion adopted by the Welsh antiquaries. Vide Cambrian Quarterly Magazine, vol. i. p. 318.

Fig. 20 ᛒᛗᛏᛁᛋᚠᛖᚾᚱ ᚹᛁᛏᛗ ᛗᚼᚻ ᛒ

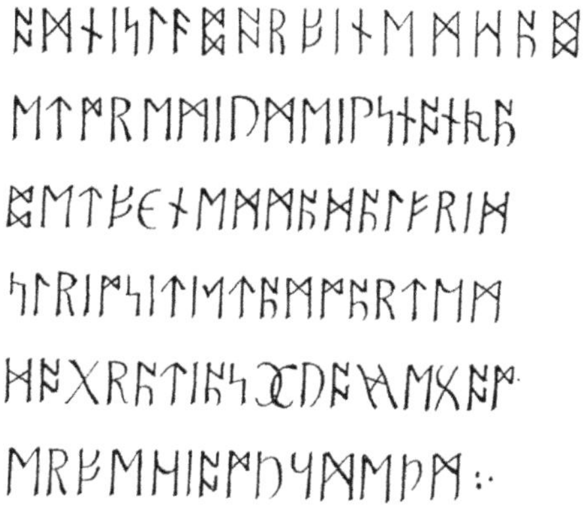

ᛗᛏ ᛒᚱᛗᛗᛁᛚᛗᛗᛁᛒᛋᚼᚦᛁᚼ

ᛒᛗᛏᚹᛖᛏᛗᛗᚼᚻᛁᛋᚠᚱᛁᚼ

ᚼᛁᚱᛁᛋᛁᛏᛁᛏᛒᛗᛗᛏᛒᚱᛏᛗᛗ

ᚼᛖᚷᚱᚻᛏᛁᛏᛋ᙭ᛞᚠᛦᛗᚷᛗᛋ

ᛗᚱᚹᛗᚼᛁᛖᛗᛑᚼᚼᛗᛏᚦᛗ ∵

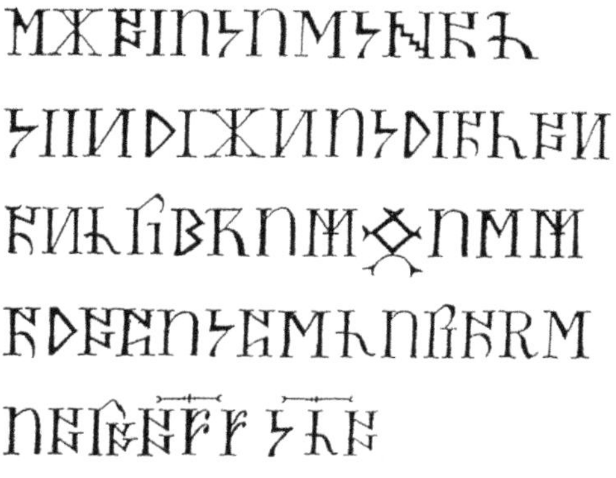

Fig. 21 ᛗᚷᛒᛁᛁᛋᛏᛑᛗᛋᚼᚻᛏ

ᛋᛁᛁᛑᛁᚷᛁᛁᛑᛋᛑᛁᚻᚻᛖᛁᛁ

ᚱᚼᛏᚻᛒᚱᛑᛗ◇ᛑᛗᛗ

ᚱᛑᛒᛁᛑᛋᚼᛗᛏᛑᚱᚱᛗ

ᛑᚻᚱᛒᚠᛦ ᛋᛏᚻᛁ

Fig. 22 ᛗᛡᚼᚠᛏᚠᚱᛁᛏ ∴

Fig. 23 ⫴Ⅺ ∶ ᚱᚠᚱᚠ ᚻᚻ ∶ ᛋᚻᚱ ∶ ᛪ ᚼ ∶ ᛏ

59

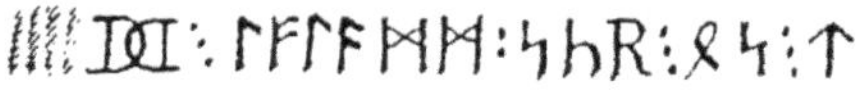

Fig. 24

The following Monuments, though in Anglo-Saxon Runes,
are not in the Anglo-Saxon language or any of its dialects.

i

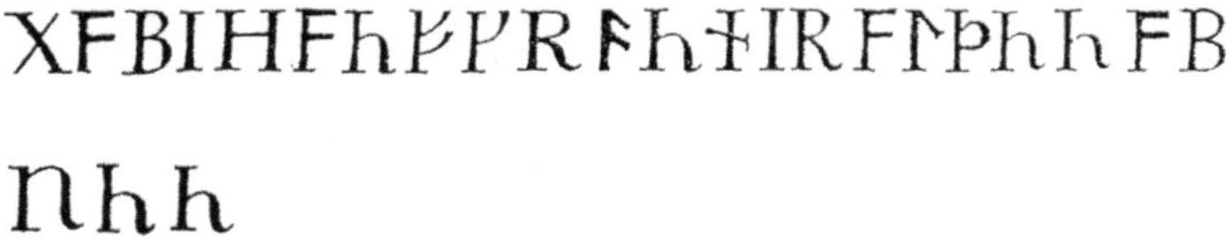

ᛝᚠᛒᛁ�ᚺᚠᚻᚹᛈᚱ ᚠᚺᛏᛁᚱᚠᚹᚦᚻᚻ ᚠᛒ

ᚢᚻᚻ

Whittaker. Richmondshire. ii. 229.

ii

ᚻᛒᛏᛈᚷᚱᚢᛁᛗᛁᚢᚹᛞ

Cott. M.S. Otho. C. S. (Hickes Thes. Gram. Isl. Tab. III.

iii

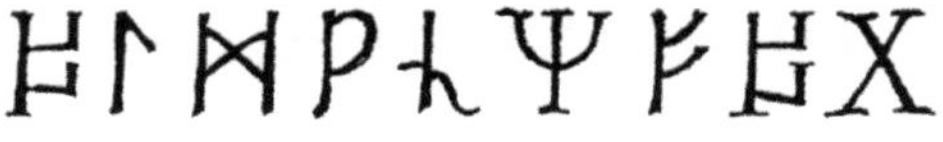

ᛡᚷᚼᛈᚹᛉᛣᚠᛒᛝ

Hickes Thes.

60

ᚠᚢᚱᛁᚲᛋᛅᚱᚦᚢᛅᚱᛆᛆᚱᚦᚢᛅᚢᚠᚢᛅᛏᛁᛁᛋᛏᚢᚦ

ᚱᚢᛁᚢᛁᚢᛁᚠᚦᚠᚱᛋᛅ ᛏᚱᚢᛏᛁᛅᛁᚢᚱᛁᚲᛋᛅᚱᚦᚢᛅᚱᛆ

ᚢᛁᚦᚱᛆᚦᚱᛆᚢᛆᚱᛁ.

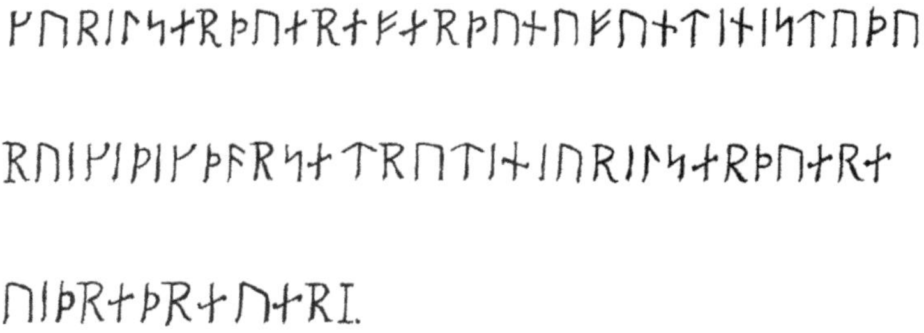

Cott. . M . S. Cal. A. XI. Hickes. Thes. Gram. Isl. Tab. VI.

ᛉ ᛘᚱᛟ·ᚱᛁ· ᚢᛂ· ᚻᚠᚱ·ᛟᚱᛚ· ᚢᚱᛁ· ᛈᚠᚱ· ᛈᛚᛙᛋ·ᛏᛙ·

ᚴᚻᛏᛙ·ᛆᚠᚱ·

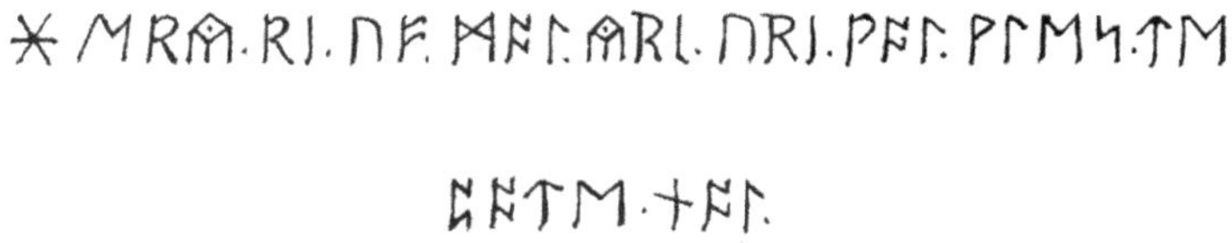

Archæologia . Vol XXI. p. 117 (1824)

ᛏ. ᚠᚱᛉᚱᛁᚢᚠ ᛙᛉᚱᛁᚢᚱᛁᚦᛂᛌᛉᛚᚠᛁᛏ ᚠᚴᛆᛏᛏᚠᚱ.

�ᛉᚱᛁᚢᚱᛁᚠᛆᛏ ᛨᛌᛚᚠᛋᛏᚠᚴᛒᛏᚠᚱ ᛨᚠᚱᛉᚱᛁᚢᚠᛙ.

Archæologia. Vol XX. p. 26. (1823)

The last document I propose to call attention to is a portion of the Anglo-Saxon poem of Salomon and Saturn, in a MS. at Corpus Christi College, Cambridge.

This contains several Runes, the use of which I shall proceed to point out.

And seðe wile geornlîce
ðone Godes cwide
singan sôðlîce,
and hine symle wile
lufian bûtan leahtrum,
he mæg ðone lâðan gâst,
feohtende feônd,
fleôndne gebringan;
gif ðû him arest on ûfan
ierne gebringest
Prologa prima
ðâm is ᛢ. P. nama:
hafað gûðmecga
gyrde lange,
gyldene gâde, and â
ðone grimman feônd
swîðmôd swâpað;
and him on swaðe fylgeð
ᚠ. A. ofermægene
and hine eâc ofslyhð.
ᛏ. T. hine teswað and hine
on ða tungan sticað,
wræstað him ðæt woddor,
ða wongan briceð:
ᛗ. E. hine yflað,
swâ he â wile
ealra feônda gehwone
fæste gestandan;
ðonne hine on unðanc ᚱ. R.
eorringa gesêceð;
bôcstafa brego
bregdeð sona
feônd be ðâm feaxe,
læteð flint brecan
scines sconcan;

[And he who wishes earnestly
the word of God
to sing truthfully
and Him would always
love without transgressions,
he can bring the evil spirit,
the warring fiend,
to flight;
if you first upon him
keenly bring down
the opening Prologue
whose name is P:
this warrior has
a lengthy rod,
a golden goad, and without pause,
the terrible fiend
he, fierce-minded, drives;
and in his trail follows
A. with real power
and strikes at him also.
T. harms him and him
in the tongue jabs,
wrings his throat
(and) his jaw breaks:
E. injures him,
as he always wishes
each of all fiends
to valliantly attack;
then R., with evil intent,
angrily seeks him out;
(this) prince of letters
quickly pulls
the fiend by his hair,
lets flint smash
the shin-bone;

he ne besceâwað nô	he does not at all show concern
his leomena lið,	for the joint of his limbs:
ne bið him lace gôd.	a doctor will do him no good.
Wendeð he hine ðonne under wolcnum,	He moves away then under the clouds,
wîgsteall sêceð,	seeks some place of defence,
heôlstre behelmed;	concealed by darkness;
huru him bið æt heortan wâ	yet in his heart there is misery
ðonne he hangiende	when, hanging there,
helle wisceð,	he yearns for hell,
ðæs engestan	that most oppressive
êðelrîces;	homeland.
ðonne hine forcinnað ðâ	Then him ?attack
ða cyrican ge tûnas;	the churches and towns[64]
[ᛉ] N. [ᚠ] O. somod	N and [?O] together,
æghwæðer bringeð	each brings him
sweôpan of sîðe;	rushing on his way;
sârgiað hwîle	for a while they torment
fremdne flaschoman,	the alien body,
feorh ne bemurnæð;	they do not feel for his life;
ðonne ᚻ . S. cymeð,	then S. comes,
engla geræswa,	leader of angels,
wuldores stæf,	letter of glory,
wrâðne gegrîpeð	seizes the angry
feônd be ðâm fôtum,	fiend by the feet,
læteð foreweard hleor	dashes his face
on strangne stân,	into a hard rock,
and stregdað tôðas	and strews his teeth
geond helle heâp:	over the crowds of hell;
hydeð hine aghwylc	each of them hides himself
æfter sceades scîman:	in the gloom of a shadow:
sceaða bið gebysigod,	the trouble-maker is afflicted,
Satanes ðegn	Satan's servant
swîðe gestilled.	harshly quieted.
Swylce hine ᚷ . Q. and ᚾ .V.	So too Q. and U.
cwealme gehnageð,	bring him low with pain,
frome folctogan	bold leaders
farað him tôgegnes;	advance upon him;

[64]MS. ða cirican getuinnas i.e. the twin churches

habbað leôht speru,
lange sceaftas,
swiðmôde sweôpan,
swenga ne wyrnað
deôrra dynta,
him bið ðæt deôfol lâð.
ðonne hine ᛁ . L.
and se yrra ᚳ . C.
gûðe begyrdað,
geâp stæf wîgeð
bîterne brogan:
bydað sona
hellehæftling
ðæt he on hinder gað:
ðonne hine ᚠ . F. and ᛗ . M.
ûtan ymbðringað
scyldigne sceaðan;
habbað scearp speru
atole earhfare;
æled lætað
on ðæs feôndes feax,
flâna stregdan
bîterne brôgan;
banan heardlîce,
grimme ongildað
ðæs hie oft gilp brecað;
ðonne hine æt niehstan
nearwe stilleð
ᚷ . G. se geâpa
ðone God sendeð
freôndum on fultum,
fǣreð æfter ᛗ . D.
fîfmægnum full:
fyr bið se ðridda
stæf stræte neâh
stille bîdeð:
[ᚾ]. H. onetteð,

they have bright spears,
long poles,
to drive him relentlessly;
they do not restrain their strokes,
severe blows:
to them the devil is hateful.
Then [I. and] L.
and the angry C.
surround him in battle,
the ?open letter [i.e. C?] attacks
the comfortless phantom:
at once turns[65]
the prisoner of hell
so that he goes backwards:
then F. and M.
press round
the guilty trouble-maker;
they have sharp spears,
vicious discharge of arrows;
they send fire
into the fiend's hair,
darts scattering
over the comfortless phanthom;
harshly they make the killer
pay terribly,
because ?he often breaks his vow;
then at length
tightly constrains him
the ?open G.,
whom God sends
to friends as a help.
Afterwards comes D.,
filled with five powers:
fire is the third
letter, by the street
he quietly waits [?=B.].
H. hurries up,

[65]MS. bigað, not bydað.

| engel hine scyrpeð | an angel (who) dresses himself, |
| on cwîcum wadum. | in living clothes.[66] B.G.] |

In this poem the Runes might have been omitted altogether without making any alteration in the sense: that is to say, they stand only for letters and not for words,as in former passages cited in this paper. Accordingly each one is accompanied by the corresponding Roman capital; and in a second copy of the same poem, in the same library, the Runes are altogether omitted, and the Roman letters stand alone. The subject matter of the lines are the powers and virtues of the paternoster, and in dilating upon these Salomon attributes certain peculiar effects to each *letter* of which the prayer is composed. Now the whole poem may be written with the following letters, variously repeated and combined: P.A.T.E.R.N.O.S.Q.U.I.C.L.F.M.G.D. and H; and these are the very Runes introduced into the poem. I however is omitted and L misplaced, from which, as well as some abruptness in the sequence of the lines, I argue that we have lost one or more couplets.

I have now examined in detail all the Runic writings which are clearly Anglo-Saxon, and which were at present accessible to me, making a very large majority, nearly all in short, of those which are known to exist. Should any others hereafter be found, I may take an opportunity of returning to them. The limits of such a paper as this have compelled me to abstain from entering upon several points closely connected with the subject of German Runes, and German mythology; still more, to refrain from any notice of the Northern Runes, which must nevertheless occupy an important

---

[66]The lines of poetry are from *Solomon and Saturn*, 84-139. At the end of the excerpt, the lines after scyrpeð (lines 139-142) should read: "Cristes cempan / on cwicum wædum / godes spyrigendes / geonges hrægles", - that is "Christ's champion, in living clothes, a good pursuer, in youthful raiment." This Christian charm employs the power of the opening words of the Lord's Prayer in Latin, Pater noster qui es in coelis, but after that the letter sequence seems to break down. The explanation that (if O and I and B are added) we have the nineteen letters necessary to write out the whole Lord's Prayer in Latin is as good a solution as any.

Some of the letters are 'bound' into the text meaningfully e.g. C and G are called geap, Q and U are linked to cwealm, G is treated in terms of its runic name gifu 'generosity, charity'. In other cases the attributes and acts of the letter seem to be arbitary or subordinate to the 'story', but could equally depend on some mystical key that the poet does not choose to hand over.

For further discussion and references see the *Anglo-Saxon Poetic Records* edition of the Minor Poems, especially the Introduction pp.1-1x.

space in any complete treatise on our heathen alphabets. My main object was I confess, to show that the Ruthwell obelisk was by no means so profound a mystery as our countrymen have been contented to believe, and that we really are not under the necessity of appealing either to Danish or German industry and ingenuity for the elucidation of our national antiquaries. In the course of my argument, I have also made it clear that a knowledge of Anglo-Saxon and its dialects, as well as familiarity with the Anglo-Saxon Runes, are qualifications without which no one can pretend to explain Anglo-Saxon inscriptions. For many of the industrious and learned antiquaries of Scandinavia I entertain the highest respect; and shall be still more ready to express it, when I find that they give up their narrow and ludicrous manner of interpreting tradition for a wider and more generous recognition of its profound meaning; when, in a word, they cease to treat the mythological and epic legends which they have, more richly indeed, but still in common with all Germanic tribes, as if they were the exclusive, ascertained, prosaic data of their own national history.

John M. Kemble

I owe some explanation to Professor Finn Magnusen, of the reson why I have refrained altogether from noticing the copy of the Ruthwell inscription, which he thinks much older than Hickes' or Gordon's, and which he says Thorkelin picked up in England. I cannot but believe that Thorkelin misled both himself and Finn Magnusen: for no one here has ever heard of such an engraving: it appears to contain just as much, and no more, than Duncan's copy now contains, which would scarcely be possible had the drawing been made a century and a half ago, when half the column was burried in the earth. The capitals on which the professor finds the words Offa, Vodo Khonmed, and Erincred, show no traces now of such characters, nor are there any Runic characters whatever on the faces of the pillar to which those capitals belong; nor do the apocryphal readings thus discovered, and which may be Danish, Pictish, or anything Finn Magnussen pleases, except Anglo-Saxon, belong to the pure Anglo-Saxon inscription on the column. In this, and very much besides, the wish seems to have been father to the thought!.

The Ruthwell Cross

In order to assist a comparison of the drawings made by Duncan, Hickes and Gordon, Figs. 17, 18 and 19 have been modified and combined on pages 68 and 69.

1. The Ruthwell Cross

Duncan

Hickes

Gordon

2. The Ruthwell Cross

Duncan   Hickes   Gordon

Some of our other titles

An Introduction to the Old English Language and its Literature
Stephen Pollington

The purpose of this general introduction to Old English is not to deal with the teaching of Old English but to dispel some misconceptions about the language and to give an outline of its structure and its literature. Here you will find an outline of the origins of the English language and its early literature. Such knowledge is essential to an understanding of the early period of English history and the present form of the language. This revised and expanded edition provides a useful guide for those contemplating embarking on a linguistic journey.

£5.95

First Steps in Old English
An easy to follow language course for the beginner
Stephen Pollington

A complete and easy to use Old English language course that contains all the exercises and texts needed to learn Old English. This course has been designed to be of help to a wide range of students, from those who are teaching themselves at home, to undergraduates who are learning Old English as part of their English degree course. The author has adopted a step-by-step approach that enables students of differing abilities to advance at their own pace. The course includes practice and translation exercises, a glossary of the words used in the course, and many Old English texts, including the *Battle of Brunanburh* and *Battle of Maldon*.

£16-95

Old English Poems, Prose & Lessons   2CD s
read by Stephen Pollington

This CD contains lessons and texts from *First Steps in Old English*.
Tracks include: 1. Deor. 2. Beowulf – The Funeral of Scyld Scefing. 3. Engla Tocyme (The Arrival of the English). 4. Ines Domas. Two Extracts from the Laws of King Ine. 5. Deniga Hergung (The Danes' Harrying) Anglo-Saxon Chronicle Entry AD997. 6. Durham 7. The Ordeal (Be ðon ðe ordales weddigaþ) 8. Wið Dweorh (Against a Dwarf) 9. Wið Wennum (Against Wens) 10. Wið Wæterælfadle (Against Waterelf Sickness) 11. The Nine Herbs Charm 12. Læcedomas (Leechdoms) 13. Beowulf's Greeting 14. The Battle of Brunanburh There is a Guide to Pronunciation and sixteen Reading Exercises

£15 2CDs - Free Old English transcript from www.asbooks.co.uk.

Wordcraft   Concise English/Old English Dictionary and Thesaurus
Stephen Pollington

Wordcraft provides Old English equivalents to the commoner modern words in both dictionary and thesaurus formats. The Thesaurus presents vocabulary relevant to a wide range of individual topics in alphabetical lists, thus making it easily accessible to those with specific areas of interest. Each thematic listing is encoded for cross-reference from the Dictionary.

The two sections will be of invaluable assistance to students of the language, as well as those with either a general or a specific interest in the Anglo-Saxon period.

£9.95

Anglo-Saxon Attitudes – A short introduction to Anglo-Saxonism
J.A. Hilton
This is not a book about the Anglo-Saxons, but a book about books about Anglo-Saxons. It describes the academic discipline of Anglo-Saxonism; the methods of study used; the underlying assumptions; and the uses to which it has been put.

Methods and motives have changed over time but right from the start there have been constant themes: English patriotism and English freedom.

£5.95 hardback 64 pages

The Origins of the Anglo-Saxons
Donald Henson
This book has three great strengths.

First, it pulls together and summarises the whole range of evidence bearing on the subject, offering an up-to-date assessment: the book is, in other words, a highly efficient introduction to the subject. Second – perhaps reflecting Henson's position as a leading practitioner of public archaeology (he is currently Education and Outreach Co-ordinator for the Council for British Archaeology) – the book is refreshingly jargon free and accessible. Third, Henson is not afraid to offer strong, controversial interpretations. The Origins of the Anglo-Saxons can therefore be strongly recommended to those who want a detailed road-map of the evidence and debates for the migration period.
Current Archaeology 2006

£18.95 296 pages

The Elder Gods – The Otherworld of Early England
Stephen Pollington
The purpose of the work is to bring together a range of evidence for pre-Christian beliefs and attitudes to the Otherworld drawn from archaeology, linguistics, literary studies and comparative mythology. The rich and varied English tradition influenced the worldview of the later mediaeval and Norse societies. Aspects of this tradition are with us still in the 21st century.

£35 70 illustrations 526 pages

A Departed Music – Readings in Old English Poetry
Walter Nash
The *readings* of this book take the form of passages of translation from some Old English poems. The author paraphrases their content and discuses their place and significance in the history of poetic art in Old English society and culture.

The author's knowledge, enthusiasm and love of his subject help make this an excellent introduction to the subject for students and the general reader.

£9.95 hardback 240 pages

Tolkien's *Mythology for England* - A Guide to Middle Earth
Edmund Wainwright
You will find here an outline of Tolkien's life and work. The main part of the book consists of an alphabetical subject list which aims to give the reader a greater understanding of Tolkien's Middle-Earth, the creatures that inhabited it and the languages they spoke. The focus is on the Lord of the Rings and how Tolkien's knowledge and enthusiasm for Anglo-Saxon and Norse literature and history helped shape its plot and characters.

£9.95 hardback

Rudiments of Runelore
Stephen Pollington

The purpose of this book is to provide both a comprehensive introduction for those coming to the subject for the first time, and a handy and inexpensive reference work for those with some knowledge of the subject. The *Abecedarium Nordmannicum* and the English, Norwegian and Icelandic rune poems are included as are two rune riddles, extracts from the Cynewulf poems and new work on the three Brandon runic inscriptions and the Norfolk 'Tiw' runes.

Include: The Origin of the Runes; Runes among the Germans; The Germanic Rune Row and the Common Germanic Language; The English Runic Tradition; The Scandinavian Runic Tradition; Runes and Pseudo-runes; The Use of Runes; Bind Runes and Runic Cryptography.

£5.95 Illustrations

Woden's Warriors
Paul Mortimer

This book explores some of the resources available to warriors in Anglo-Saxon England and northern Europe during the 6th and 7th centuries. In this time of great change, the remains of old empires were still visible but new ideas and methods of organisation were making possible the growth of centralised kingdoms which became the nation states that dominated Europe for the next thousand years.

It was also a time of great artistry and wealth, much of which was devoted to the creation of works of art devoted to war and warfare. It is a time when traditional symbols of identity and the old gods were mingling with new patterns of belief.

This book provides the reader with glimpses of what it was like to be part of a warrior society.

Over 300 illustrations

£45 305 illustrations large format hardback 304 pages

Wayland's Work – Anglo-Saxon Art 4th to 7th century
Stephen Pollington

Not only was there considerable artistry in the output of early Anglo-Saxon workshops, but it was vigorous, complex and technically challenging.

The designs found on Anglo-Saxon artefacts are never mere ornament: in a society which used visual and verbal signals to demonstrate power, authority, status and ethnicity, no visual statement was ever empty of meaning.

The aim of this work is to prompt a better understanding of Anglo-Saxon art and the society which produced it. Nothing like this has been published for nearly 100 years.

£70 548 pages 62 colour plates, 226 illustrations

Anglo-Saxon Books
Order online at www.asbooks.co.uk
Check website for changes in prices and availability

Organisations

Þa Engliscan Gesiðas

Þa Engliscan Gesiðas is a historical and cultural society exclusively devoted to Anglo-Saxon history. The Fellowship publishes a quarterly journal, *Wiðowinde,* and has a website with regularly updated information and discussions. Local groups arrange their own meetings and attend lectures, exhibitions and events. Members are able to share their interest with like-minded people and learn more about the origins and growth of English culture, including language, literature, archaeology, anthropology, architecture, art, religion, mythology, folklore and material culture.

For further details see   www.tha-engliscan-gesithas.org.uk   or write to:
Membership Secretary,   The English Companions, PO Box 62790, London, SW12 2BH, England

Regia Anglorum

Regia Anglorum is an active group of enthusiasts who attempt to portray as accurately as possible the life and times of the people who lived in the British Isles around a thousand years ago. We investigate a wide range of crafts and have a Living History Exhibit that frequently erects some thirty tented period structures.

Our site at Wychurst has a large Anglo-Saxon hall – defended manor house - which has been reconstructed using the best available evidence. Members can learn weapon skills with accurate copies of weapons of the period. We own and operate six full scale vessels ranging from a 6 metre Faering to a 15 metre ocean-going trader!

We have a thriving membership and 40 branches in the British Isles and United States - so there might be one near you. We especially welcome families with children.
   www.regia.org   *General information* eolder@regia.org   *Membership* join@regia.org

The Sutton Hoo Society

Our aims and objectives focus on promoting research and education relating to the Anglo Saxon Royal cemetery at Sutton Hoo, Suffolk in the UK. The Society publishes a newsletter SAXON twice a year, which keeps members up to date with society activities, carries resumes of lectures and visits, and reports progress on research and publication associated with the site. If you would like information about membership see website: www.suttonhoo.org

Wuffing Education

Wuffing Education provides those interested in the history, archaeology, literature and culture of the Anglo-Saxons with the chance to meet experts and fellow enthusiasts for a whole day of in-depth seminars and discussions. Day Schools take place at the historic Tranmer House overlooking the burial mounds of Sutton Hoo in Suffolk. For details events go to -
   website www.wuffings.co.uk email education@wuffings.co.uk

Places to visit

Bede's World at Jarrow

Bede's world tells the remarkable story of the life and times of the Venerable Bede, 673–735 AD. Visitors can explore the origins of early medieval Northumbria and Bede's life and achievements through his own writings and the excavations of the monasteries at Jarrow and other sites.

Location – 10 miles from Newcastle upon Tyne, off the A19 near the southern entrance to the River Tyne tunnel. Bus services 526 & 527

Bede's World, Church Bank, Jarrow, Tyne and Wear, NE32 3DY

Tel. 0191 489 2106; Fax: 0191 428 2361; website: www.bedesworld.co.uk

Sutton Hoo near Woodbridge, Suffolk

Sutton Hoo is a group of low burial mounds overlooking the River Deben in south-east Suffolk. Excavations in 1939 brought to light the richest burial ever discovered in Britain – an Anglo-Saxon ship containing a magnificent treasure which has become one of the principal attractions of the British Museum. The mound from which the treasure was dug is thought to be the grave of Rædwald, an early English king who died in 624/5 AD.

This National Trust site has an excellent visitor centre, which includes a reconstruction of the burial chamber and its grave goods. Some original objects as well as replicas of the treasure are on display.

2 miles east of Woodbridge on B1083   Tel. 01394 389700

West Stow Anglo-Saxon Village

An early Anglo-Saxon Settlement reconstructed on the site where it was excavated consisting of timber and thatch hall, houses and workshop. There is also a museum containing objects found during the excavation of the site. Open all year 10am (except Christmas) Last entrance summer 4pm; winter 3-30pm. Special provision for school parties. A teachers' resource pack is available. Costumed events are held on some weekends, especially Easter Sunday and August Bank Holiday Monday. Craft courses are organised.

For further details see www.weststow.org or contact:

The Visitor Centre, West Stow Country Park, Icklingham Road, West Stow,

Bury St Edmunds, Suffolk IP28 6HG   Tel. 01284 728718

Lightning Source UK Ltd.
Milton Keynes UK
UKHW021854050920
369410UK00008B/123

9 781898 281634